¡Palabra!

Black Identity in the Literature of the Spanish Caribbean

Diana Pardo, Ph.D.

blue ocean press

tokyo

Published by:

blue ocean press, an imprint of Aoishima Research Institute
#807-36 Lions Plaza Ebisu
3-25-3 Higashi, Shibuya-ku
Tokyo, Japan 150-0011

Email: contact@blueoceanpublications.com
URL: http://www.blueoceanpublications.com

ISBN: 978-4-902837-49-0

Table of Contents

Chapter 1
Introduction[1]

In the last thirty years Spanish-Caribbean literature has focused on the theme of black identity as an expression of racial pride. This expression counteracts the stereotypical images of blacks in earlier works such as: *Sab* (1841) by Gertrudis Gómez de Avellaneda, *Cecilia Valdés* (1882) by Cirilo Villaverde, and *María* (1867) by Jorge Isaacs (among others), which depict docile blacks dwelling in the suffering and humiliation of mental bondage. The absence of images in these early works that portray blacks as worthy or dignified manifests a sense of self-hate based on the traditional colonialist order. Nevertheless, as different ideological and aesthetic trends evolve, so does the intellectual consciousness of contemporary writers who challenge the prevailing and existing features of traditional critics. For example, writers such as Ana Lydia Vega (1946) from Puerto Rico, Blas Jiménez (1948) from the Dominican Republic, and Nancy Morejón (1944) from Cuba, have conscientiously and progressively concentrated on a new racial reality that depicts a more believable

---

[1] Frantz Fanon, *The Wretched of the Earth*, (New York: Grove Press, 1963) 240.

portrayal of blacks in the Spanish-speaking Caribbean.

Through their work these artists confront and defy the "monolithic and homogeneous" [2] canon and promote what West calls the "new politics of difference," as he explains:

> Distinctive features of the new cultural politics of difference are to trash the monolithic and homogenous in the name of diversity, multiplicity and heterogeneity; to reject the abstract, general and universal in lighting the contingent, provisional, variable, tentative, shifting and changing. Needless to say, these gestures are not new in the history of criticism or art, yet what makes them novel—along with the cultural politics they produce—is how and what constitutes difference, the weight and gravity it is given in representation, and the way in which highlighting issues like exterminism, empire, class, race, gender, sexual orientation, age, nation, nature and region at this historical moment acknowledges some discontinuity and disruption from previous forms of cultural critique. To put it bluntly, the new cultural politics of difference consists of creative responses to the precise circumstances of our present moment— especially those of marginalized First World agents who shun degraded self-representations, articulating

---

[2] (West 3)

instead their sense of the flow of history in light of the contemporary terrors, anxieties and fears of highly commercialized North Atlantic capitalist cultures (with their escalating xenophobias against people of color, Jews, women, gays, lesbians and the elderly). [3]

The purpose of this research is to examine the theme of black identity, with an emphasis on pride, in order to counteract the portrayal of black images as negative stereotypes. We demonstrate how writers Ana Lydia Vega, in her collection of short stories *Encancaranublado y otros cuentos de naufragio* (1994), Blas Jiménez, in his collection of poems *Caribe africano en despertar* (1984), and Nancy Morejón, in her collection of poems *Where the Island Sleeps Like a Wing* (1985), humanize the image of blacks by illustrating different aspects and dimensions of the black psyche in Spanish-speaking Caribbean islands. In order to elucidate what these authors are trying to accomplish, we will examine the above-mentioned texts with the purpose of showing how Vega, Jiménez, and Morejón represent the silenced voices through "creative responses to the precise circumstances of our present moment..."[4], as they address the absence of authentic characterization of blacks.

---

[3] (West 4)

[4] (West 4)

For instance, in the analysis of Vega's short stories "Encancaranublado" and "El día de los hechos" from the collection *Encancaranublado y otros cuentos de naufragio*, we apply the concepts established by Walter J. Ong in Orality and Literacy: The Technologizing of the Word (1982). The first "conservative and traditionalist,"[5] requires the repeating of traditions in order that they may be kept alive. The retelling of stories is a variation of the original story, that is, the new story although based on the initial one will be told in a unique fashion more appropriate and current with the time. The other "close reference to the human lifeworld,"[6] stems from an oral culture that relays occurrences that arise from personal experiences. The person telling the story has been closely related to the events, therefore, the accounts of these will be considered dependable.

Moreover, we refer to the text Kafka: Toward a Minor Literature (1986) by Gilles Deleuze and Felix Guattari and utilize their theory of a minor literature. They state that "deterritorialization," "the connection of the individual and the political," and the "collective value," (16–27) are characteristics of the theory of a minor literature. They are

---

[5] (Ong 41)

[6] (Ong 42)

used by members of a minority group within a dominant language for the creation of a style alien to that of the standard. The deterritorialization of the language demands that one step outside the realms of the dominant language and invent a style uncommon to that of the standard, but recognizable by those of that minority group. The creation of this style offers another possibility of expression for that particular group, as is evident in the stories by Vega.

Deleuze and Guattari theorize that the characteristic "the connection of the individual and the political," stresses that everything in a minor literature is affiliated with the political due to its limited space. As a result, literature takes on an entirely new meaning. They also claim that "what in great literature goes on down below, constituting a not indispensable cellar of the structure, here takes place in the full light of day, what is there a matter of passing interest for a few, here absorbs everyone no less than as a matter of life and death"[7]. They insist that the last characteristic of a minor literature, "collective value":

> is literature that produces an active solidarity in spite of skepticism; and if the writer is in the margins or completely outside his or her fragile community, this situation allows the writer all the more the possibility

---

[7] (Deleuze and Guattari 17)

to express another possible community and forge the means for another consciousness and another sensibility.[8]

The interest in these characteristics rests on their manifestion in the works of Vega, whose prose challenges the traditional roles born of the influences of the dominant order.

In our examination of Jiménez's poems from the collection *Caribe africano en despertar*, we implement Josaphat B. Kubayanda's theory, as presented in *The Poet's Africa: Africaness in the Poetry of Nicolás Guillén and Aimé Césaire* (1990),[9] because he defines the journey of the colonized as stages that eventually lead to attainment of consciousness, and because we observe the interaction of the four stages in Jiménez's collection of poems. The four stages of the journey, as interpreted by Kubayanda, are: "stoicism,

---

[8] (Deleuze and Guattari 17)

[9] Kubayanda interprets George F. W. Hegel's theories in the chapter "Lordship and Bondage" in *The Phenomenology of the Spirit*, (1817). Based on this reading, Kubayanda claims "Hegel discounted Africa from world history out of complete ignorance of Africa's role in antiquity and in human development before the modern European 'Discovery.' However, in a broad sense, his idealistic theory of recognition was perceived to be applicable to the historical fact of colonization and enslavement (lordship) and the history of slave resistance and emancipation (bondage)" (Kubayanda 37).

skepticism, unhappy consciousness, and rational consciousness." (36–37) It must be noted, however, that the concept of "stoicism," or the acceptance of the oppressed condition, is rarely observed in the poetry of Jiménez. Jiménez minimizes this stage in his poems because of its moment of inactivity and because it represents the subservience of the oppressed. Attention to this stage would signify the acceptance and perpetuation of the idea of passivity. On the contrary, the poems project a discourse that encourages change; the poems do not sketch, depict, or suggest passivity or subservience.

Saidiya V. Hartman's theory from the text Scenes of Subjection: Terror, Slavery, and Self-Making in Nineteenth-Century America (1997), centers on the violent institution of slavery, which displaced blacks through captivity and, as a result, fostered an attitude of rebellion, an attitude that offers relief from the stress of the rigors of enslavement and oppression. In the analysis of the poems by Morejón of the collection Where the Island Sleeps Like a Wing, we apply the following three concepts, "memory and history," "embodied needs and the politics of hunger," and "redress." (49–78) The first concept "memory and history," delves into the history of violence and explicates how its rupture obliged slaves to attenuate the pain through articulation and resistance.

The second concept, "embodied needs and the politics of hunger," manifests itself through the juba song, a vernacular form that serves as entertainment and critiques the masters, the system of slavery or the dominant forces in order to affect redress. The final concept, "redress," heals the pained body of the enslaved. The means of healing are multiple and may vary; the ultimate form of redress for the purpose of this chapter configures the resistant element that eventually leads to the Cuban Revolution.

Not as recognizable within the spheres of the traditional canon, the works of Vega, Jiménez, and Morejón, contribute significantly to Afro-Caribbean letters, because they espouse distinct articulations representative of their cultural, racial, and national background. The selection of these writers for the analysis of this research lies in that each consistently challenges and attempts to reconstruct images formulated by the existing criteria. Uniquely and responsibly, each defaces the negative self-image by confronting stereotypes and myths rooted in history. That is, each writer's treatment of the issue although different, disputes, and contests the existing criteria used for the creation and perpetuation of these negative images.

Vega's works manage issues of the disenfranchised and in general the social and cultural problems that surround the Caribbean islands. She engages her characters in and gender stereotypical settings in order to reveal their hardships and dilemmas. Known for her innovative language that embodies the popular culture, at times, she combines English and Spanish to reflect the North American presence in the Caribbean. Among her works are the collections of short stories *Vírgenes y mártires* (1981), *Pasión de historia y otras historias de pasión* (1987), *Falsas crónicas del sur* (1991), and a collection of essays *El tramo ancla: ensayos puertorriqueños de hoy* (1988). Chiefly, the writer's concern centers on the people, the history, and the commonality among the people of the Caribbean islands, as she grasps the attention of the reader and makes an appeal for the restitution of a common bond.

For instance, in the short stories that we analyze, "Encancaranublado" and "El día de los hechos," Vega reproduces the defects and squabbles common to the people of Haiti, Puerto Rico, Dominican Republic, and Cuba, in order to demonstrate the need for regional unity. By addressing the issues of present day society, the writer gains the reader's trust and establishes a relationship between the text and the reader. Simultaneously, she refutes the traditional order by illustrating the various negative images internalized by the people.

The language of Vega's prose is permeated with Caribbean popular culture representative of the festive spirit that embodies the soul of the people in spite of their condition. The exemplarary morsels of cultural identity in her stories reflect the reality and experiences of the people in the Spanish–speaking Caribbean. To inform a new sensibility representative of that geographical area, Vega recreates negative but realistic scenarios reflective of that particular culture, and deconstructs the psyche originally forged by the Spanish colonial society.

Similarly, Jiménez in his collection of poems *Caribe africano en despertar*, (1984) presents a literature that inspires the deracination of the image of the oppressor. He advocates the replacement of this negative image with one that strives for the dismissal of the influences that continue to torment Dominican society. His effort to authenticate the black presence of the country through his poetry also pervades in his other collections of poems, *Aquí otro español* (1980), and *Exigencias de un cimarrón (en sueños)* (1987). Jiménez is one of the few Dominican poets besides Norberto James well versed in Spanish and English, who places black identity at the forefront of his works. His deft management of the theme of identity, as it reflects societal issues, unswervingly asserts and affirms black pride.

Unlike Vega who utilizes the popular Spanish language of the Caribbean, as well as English, in the stories we analyze, Jiménez employs the standard Spanish language to oppose and correct the stereotypes and racial myths that informed the psyche of the Dominican people. The language evidences the need for personal introspection on the part of the people, for the purpose of renouncing negative values previously established. In Minority Discourse and the African Collective: Some Examples from Latin American and Caribbean Literature (1985), Kubayanda explicates, "maroon literature":

> The maroon text's commitment to the principle of full emancipation constantly comes to the fore through a language that contradicts the textural and political claims of the old raison d'etat, or those of the nascent criollo superstructure. [10]

Jiménez advocates black identity through the acknowledgement of self–history, for instance, the cimarrón, the runaway slave, embodies the quintessential manifestation of freedom. Jiménez, who dedicates the collection of poems *Caribe africano en despertar*, to his grandfather, himself a cimarrón, distinguishes the cimarrón, as the original prototype of freedom and a model from which to pattern

---

[10] (Kubayanda 126)

thoughts of liberation and self-expression.

Furthermore, he discloses the prevailing flaws in "nascent criollo superstructure"[11] for instance, black self-denial, an issue that torments the psyche of the Dominican Republic, in order to point out the need for an appropriation of these models for the purpose of self-enlightenment and self-identification. For example, for Jiménez, the outlandish use of "Indio" (Indian) on Dominican passports for racial identification discloses the origins of the formulation of the pessimistic image.[12]

These negative and positive representations purposefully encourage introspection and stimulate retrospection to produce a healthy self-esteem. The correlation of divergent viewpoints or of meditation encourages the necessary self-analysis and evaluation in order to stimulate the reconstruction of black identity.

In comparison with Vega and Jiménez, Nancy Morejón tenaciously endeavors to uplift and authenticate the

---

[11] (Kubayanda 126)

[12] Jiménez... consider[s] it a racist attempt to render Dominican Blacks officially invisible... some people resist Black Dominicans calling themselves Black because if they do, that would mean others would have to admit that they too, are Black. (qtd in Jackson 89)

black self-image. Like them, Morejón unwaveringly struggles to dispose of the denigrated self-image of blacks in Cuba. Morejón, who was born in Havana, studied French in The Universidad de La Habana. Her research thesis focused on Aimé Césaire, the Martiniquen who studied negritude from a Francophone perspective. She has translated his works as well as other Francophone writers such as Jacque Roumain and René Depestre. Some of her other collections of poems are: *Mutismos* (1962), *Amor, ciudad atribuida* (1964), *Richard trajo su flauta y otros argumentos* (1967), *Parajes de una época* (1979), *Octubre imprescindible* (1982), *Cuaderno de Granada* (1984), *La quinta de los molinos* (2000). Morejón's works have been translated to French, English, Polish, Italian, Portuguese, Russian, and Dutch, and her repertoire also includes literary essays, including Nación y mestizaje en Nicolás Guillén (1982).

Morejón's work, *Where the Island Sleeps Like a Wing*, a bilingual collection of poems contains models that inspire optimism and hope. These models may recall historical figures that epitomize strength and courage as they transform their condition of oppression. The historical aspect serves as a source of accessible positive information for the oppressed people to utilize in order to overcome their plight.

Like Vega and Jiménez, Morejón manipulates language to acquaint her reader with a distinct perspective representative of black culture. However, Morejón utilizes a reversal of the language to reeducate a collective customarily resigned to the format established by the dominant order. She makes adjustments in language, whose:

> function is clearly one of reversal at the level of speech; however, it also raises and nurtures a combative consciousness through linguistic subversiveness. Here its function is the affirmation of the roots of a minority culture. It has a collective value because its goal is to arouse and nourish a collective sensibility. [13]

For example, the poem "Negro" nullifies the idea of white aesthetics by regarding these disagreeable features as the sentiments and definition of others: "tu pelo / para algunos / era diablura del infierno."[14] On one hand, the poem reveals the origins of white aesthetics imposed on blacks by "others," and on the other, the language employed by Morejón attempts to expunge these beliefs. In essence, these contemporary writers, Vega, Jiménez, and Morejón conscientiously and progressively concentrate on a new racial reality that pictures a more accurate portrayal of

---

[13] (Kubayanda 119)

[14] (Morejón 72)

blacks.[15]

Significantly they question the national values that shaped the thought of Caribbean society, as they humanize the image of blacks by depicting real and legitimate dimensions of the black psyche in the Spanish-speaking Caribbean islands. Franz Fanon in The Wretched of the Earth (1961), claims that:

> while at the beginning the native intellectual used to produce his work to be read exclusively by the oppressor, whether with intention of charming him or denouncing him through ethical or subjectivist means, now the native writer progressively takes on the habit of addressing his own people. It is only from that moment that we can speak of a national lite[4]rature. Here there is, at the level of literary creation, the taking up and clarification of themes that are typically

----

[15] The new cultural politics of difference is neither simply oppositional in contesting the mainstream (or malestream) for inclusion nor transgressive in the avant-gardist sense of shocking conventional bourgeois audiences. It embraces the distinct articulations of talented (and usually privileged) contributors to culture who desire to align themselves with demoralized, demobilized, depoliticized and disorganized people in order to empower and enable social action and, if possible, to enlist collective insurgency for the expansion of their production, the very operations of power within their immediate work contexts (academy, museum, gallery, mass media). (West 4)

<blockquote>
nationalist. This may be properly called a literature of combat, in the sense that it calls upon the whole people to fight for their existence as a nation.[16]
</blockquote>

These writers of the "new cultural politics of difference" (West) through articulation seek to grasp, embody, and incorporate the unequivocal cultural qualities, first and foremost, for national acceptance and inclusion. Their literature counteracts the black images in earlier works in which blacks played stereotypical roles. Considered "maroon literature"[17] these works have roots in a "guerrilla resistance movement"[18], which challenges the system of the dominant order. This literature evades the canon's criteria and resorts to one that reflects the distinctive aspects that have shaped the black psyche in the Caribbean.

---

[16] (Fanon 240)

[17] (Kubayanda 124)

[18] (Kubayanda 124)

Chapter 2
"Encancaranublado" Disclosed

Resolver el problema después de conocer sus elementos, es más fácil que
resolver el problema sin conocerlos.... Conocer es resolver.
– Martí [19]

Puerto Rican writer Ana Lydia Vega assumes the responsibility of "addressing [her] own people"[20]. To address her people effectively she sets out to narrow the gap between the text and the reader. She skillfully, methodically, and efficiently resorts to tackling national issues fundamentally rooted in colonialism for the sake of clarifying misconceptions. Vega said:

> esta generación de escritores los que surgieron de los setenta ha echado mano de elementos de la cultura popular muy importantes, entre ellos la música, el humor, el baile, el lenguaje festivo, la santería, el espiritismo; todo lo popular ha sido aprovechado para decir el país, para construir la cultura nacional. Estos elementos son tan importantes, son experiencias tan vigentes y auténticas que nos hemos sentido integrados

---

[19] José Martí, *Nuestra América*, (Philadelphia: Westminster Press, 1970) 17.

[20] (Fanon 240)

a ellos, como partícipes más que observadores. [21]

In her collection of short stories *Encancaranublado y otros cuentos de naufragio*, more specifically in the stories "El día de los hechos" and "Encancaranublado," we notice that Vega, as:

> the storyteller, gives free rein to [her] imagination [she] makes innovations and [she] creates a work of art. The storyteller replies to the expectant people by successive approximations, and makes [her] way, apparently alone but in fact helped on by [her] public, toward the seeking out of new patterns, that is to say national patterns. [22]

With this in mind, we illustrate how Vega manipulates her literary skills to attract the attention of her audience by appealing to the idiosyncrasies of her people. Divided into three sections, the first section of this chapter will briefly explain Ong's applicable concepts. The two concepts "conservative and traditionalist," and "close reference to the human lifeworld" are of particular interest for the purpose of this chapter, because the manifestation of these elements reveals the manipulation of the audience by

---

[21] (Vega 314)

[22] (Fanon 240)

the author. For example, Vega attracts the attention of her audience, gains their trust, and invites them to participate in the stories. This section will also illustrate Deleuze and Guattari's characteristics "deterritorialization," "connection of the individual and the political," and "the collective value,"[23] because they are evident in the stories to be analyzed. Finally, in this section we will provide a brief history of Santería in the Spanish-speaking Caribbean because of its significant appearance in "Encancaranublado" and of major importance for the purpose of our analysis.

The second section illustrates how Vega treats the issue of self-deprecation, a trait rooted in colonialism. The story "El día de los hechos" deals with a historical event that has origins in the racism reflective of the colonialist epoch's emphasis on white superiority. We demonstrate how she manipulates her reader's attention through the application of Ong's concepts of orality. She establishes a relationship between text and reader for the purpose of gaining his/her trust. In the third section, we invite the reader of the "africanía" to decode and decipher the traces of Santería extant in the story "Encancaranublado."[24] María Carmen

---

[23] These characteristics will be explained later.

[24] "Africanía" is defined by Zielina as "los elementos procedentes de la cultura africana, que llevados a la ficción se convierten en una red de

Zielina maintains in *La africanía en el cuento cubano y puertorriqueño* (1994):

> aplico el término "africanía" específicamente a la literatura, fuera de las ciencias sociales, teniendo en cuenta el papel de "sistema de códigos" que la cultura africana ha tenido para los escritores caribeños, convirtiéndolos en "masters of these codes."[25]

I. Elements of Orality and of "A Minor Literature"

When Ong writes of oral cultures his primary concern rests on a culture "untouched by writing"[26]. Since an oral culture does not have books it relies on the articulation of words. Words and sound for these cultures possess "magical potency,"[27] that is, "… all sound, and especially oral utterance, which comes from inside living organisms, is dynamic"[28]. They have the ability to capture

---

sofisticados códigos y símbolos que marcan el relato de un escritor." (Zielina 16)

[25] (Zielina 15)

[26] (Ong 31)

[27] (Ong 32)

[28] (Ong 32)

and retain the attention of an audience with a great degree persuasion. Consequently, a storyteller can manipulate an audience with a particular story for a desired reaction. Ong says that narration is not just the facility of creating a story in a unique setting or the managing of the communication exchange between the storyteller and the audience, but the adeptness to get the audience to respond. For instance, the storytellers' efforts lie in the manipulation of the audience to arouse a response. Keeping this in mind, we rely and apply some of his established characteristics of orality to Vega's stories.

The concept, "conservative and traditionalist"[29] exhibits the conservation of habits and customs of the wise old men and women who were trained to preserve these. This does not mean that the telling of an old story must be in the same manner as it was told years ago, it might be told repeatedly in various forms with new elements and in unparalleled fashion. Religious themes may be implemented variantly for the purpose of satisfying a disappointment with a particular practice; however, they "... are presented as fitting the traditions of the ancestors"[30]. Ultimately the aim is to affect the audience; the manner in which a story narrates

---

[29] (Ong 41–42)

[30] (Ong 42)

its events determines the feedback of the audience.

The second concept that we refer to, "close reference to the human lifeworld,"[31] attests the proximity of events occurred. As the antithesis of writing culture which distance[s] and in a way denature[s] the human"[32], this characteristic's point of reference counts on the people who have lived the experiences. That is, observation, involvement, and eyewitness accounts become dependable and fundamental trustworthy information.[33]

To emphasize credibility the oralist counts on communal familiarity such as formulaic expressions and other identifiable elements that bond a community to elicit a response.

In studying the works of Franz Kafka, Deleuze and Guattari have observed three characteristics that define a "minor literature." This literature expresses a discourse in a

---

[31] (Ong 42–43)

[32] (Ong 43)

[33] In the absence of elaborate analytic categories that depend on writing to structure knowledge at a distance from lived experience, oral cultures must conceptualize and verbalize all their knowledge with more or less close references to the human lifeworld, assimilating the alien, objective world to the more immediate, familiar interaction of human beings. (Ong 42)

major language by a minority group. Utilized by "an oppressive minority that speaks a language cut off from the masses,"[34] it appeals culturally to the oppressed group that inhabits the land of the oppressive dominant. The goal of this literature is to experiment within the cultural realms of a particular group. They believe that the language should be "push[ed] toward a deterritorialization... that will be an absolute deterritorialization, even if it is slow, sticky, coagulated. To bring language slowly progressively to the desert. To use syntax in order to cry, to give a syntax to the cry."[35]

The first characteristic, "deterritorialization"[36] uses the dominant language for the creation of a style alien to that of the standard; an example of this would be "what blacks today can do with the American tongue"[37]. The language is shoved to another confine that removes it from that of its original point of communication. For instance, Deleuze and Guattari insist that Kafka, writing in a Prague German, thrust the language beyond the realms of the German language to induce the oppressive qualities and underdevelopment that

---

[34] (Deleuze and Guattari 16)

[35] (Deleuze and Guattari 26)

[36] (Deleuze and Guattari 16–27)

[37] (Deleuze and Guattari 16)

the language imposed on the Czech Jews. As a result, the language of a "minor literature" expresses other particularities and idiosyncracies that on the one hand protest the injustices of dominant culture and major language. On the other hand, it creates a new utterance filled with intensities relative and representative to those of the minority group.

These intensities within the language usually take on a political agenda, which brings us to the other characteristic of a "minor literature." The second characteristic, "connection of the individual and the political"[38] stresses "a minor literature is completely different: because it exists in a narrow space, every individual matter is immediately plugged into the political"[39]. Because of limited space, all elements of the community become political and "the question of the individual becomes even more necessary, indispensable because an entirely different story stirs within it"[40]. Different from a major literature, which has the luxury of expressing individual concerns, for instance, "familial" or "marital," a "minor literature" does not have that same luxury because the attention and interest rests on other

---

[38] (Deleuze and Guattari 18–19)

[39] (Deleuze and Guattari 10)

[40] (Deleuze and Guattari 16)

responsibilities:

> its cramped space forces each individual intrigue to connect immediately to politics. The individual concern thus becomes all the more necessary, indispensable, magnified, because a whole other story is vibrating within it. In this way, the family triangle connects to other triangles—commercial, economic, bureaucratic, juridical—that determines its value. [41]

The third characteristic, "collective value,"[42] takes on the concerns of the entire minority community. Deleuze and Guattari claim that a "scarcity of talent" within this community obliges the individual the task of addressing issues that affect that particular group. Further, they insist that this "scarcity" benefits that particular group because the enunciation by an individual comprises the needs of the collective, this literature cannot be separated from the people.

> But... because collective or national consciousness is 'often inactive in external life and always in the process of breakdown,' literature finds itself positively charged with the role and function of collective, and

---

[41] (Deleuze and Guattari 17)

[42] (Deleuze and Guattari 16–27)

even revolutionary enunciation.[43]

Our objective is to illustrate the attributes of Ong's and Deleuze and Guattari's characteristics manifested in the selected short stories by Ana Lydia Vega. The application of these elements may appear independent of each other but, in some cases, they will be integrated with Ong's characteristics, either because they are interrelated and/or simply to substantiate a given point.

---

[43] (Deleuze and Guattari 17)

II. The Survival of Yoruba Elements in Santería

For various reasons African religious elements (Santería and Voodoo) survived in the Caribbean.[44] The chief reason was the landholder's failure to acknowledge the depth of the African slave's ties to ancestral beliefs, rituals, and practices. The landholder so consumed with the production of the slaves failed to realize the participation of slaves in Christian ceremonies and rituals was a disguising of their own religious practices. María Carmen Zielina adds:

> por estas razones, tanto en Cuba como en Puerto Rico, gobierno y hacendados miraban con "buenos ojos" la práctica cultural de cantos, vestimentas y adornos, que desplegaban los esclavos en determinados días, como por ejemplo el día de los Reyes Magos, o el de Santiago de Compostela, o el de cualquier otro

---

[44] Migene González-Wippler says "en Haiti, el culto del vudú fue propagado por los nagos, ibos, aradas, dahomeyanos y otras tribus. En las colonias españolas y portuguesas epecialmente Cuba y Brasil, los yorubas y bantúes trasmitieron ritos mágicos semejantes. Aunque algunos de los rituales y ceremonias de la santería no son diferentes de ritos del vudú haitiano, las divergencias son marcadas, pues no solamente estuvieron implicadas en los dos movimientos..., sino que también Haiti se encontraba bajo influencia francesa durante el tráfico de esclavos, mientras otros países del Caribe, como Cuba, Puerto Rico y la República Dominicana estaban bajo el dominio español" (González-Wippler 13).

<blockquote>
santo religioso. El colono aceptaba esta práctica cultural porque la consideraba como una vávula emocional para los esclavos; pensaba que era inofensiva y además resultaba al final una forma de halagar su narcisismo de colono; éste se autorreconocía y autohalagaba como persona generosa y cristiana.[45]
</blockquote>

Of course, after the Haitian revolution the slaves bore the brunt of bitter transformation. Haiti gained its independence from France in 1804; as a result, and the colonialist powers in the Americas considered this independence a threat to their colonies. The treatment of slaves became more cruel, austere, and inhumane as fear of uprisings increased. Nevertheless, the slaves continued to practice their religion under the guise of the master's religion.[46] From the fusion and interaction of different Yoruba beliefs combined with Catholic beliefs, Santería is born.[47]

---

[45] (Zielina 24)

[46] The Yorubas of Nigeria and other areas of West Africa brought along their myths, rituals, and beliefs to Latin America when they came as slaves. The Yoruba tribe comprised several ethnic groups, which extended to Benin. When the Ewe tribe invaded Dahomey, many were forced to leave for the coast where later the slave traders captured them. (González–Whippler)

[47] These are the phenomena of acculturation that may signify the substitution of some elements for others without becoming effective

The deities in Santería are called Orishas and the most known Obatalá, Changó, Yemaya, Eleggua, Ogun, Orunla, and Oyá constitute the Siete Potencias Africanas. The Orishas represent and control all facets of human life. Each possess special powers and although worshipped individually, together as a group they possess insurmountable power. Syncretized as Christian saints; for instance, Obatalá as Our Lady of Lourdes and Changó as Saint Barbara, and even if slaves identified the Catholic saints with the Orishas, González-Wippler claims, "para el devoto católico, la imagen de un santo es la representación ideológica.... Para el santero, o practicante de la santería, la imagen católica es la personificación de un dios Yoruba." [48] Nevertheless, combining and reconciling different elements allows "syncretism [as] the most complete intellectual manifestation of cultural mixing")[49].

---

agents of transformation of the social structure and of behavioral values within the various institutions. (Esteva-Fabregat 5)

[48] (González-Wippler 13)

[49] "syncretism [as] the most complete intellectual manifestation of cultural mixing" (Esteva-Fabregat 6)

III. The Negative Self-image

Vega contrives a literature that suggests avoiding colonial values. By exposing the denigrated self-image of blacks in her stories, she aims to deconstruct the colonial psyche of the people. Fanon attributes this psyche to the internalization of the oppressor's image, internalization evident in various aspects of the Caribbean society, a fact that leads to the perpetuation of his behavior and attitude. That is, following the code of conduct already established by the oppressor, the oppressed assimilates to their abject behavior even executing it with more violence and intensity. Vega understands clearly:

> that the function of the writer is not to be alienated
> from the reality in which he lives, but on the contrary
> to face up to the reality of that time and space which
> was allotted to him. As a writer, he must observe its
> multiple contradictions so as to arrive at a profound
> truth.[50]

She interweaves issues that reflect present day society in the Spanish-speaking Caribbean. To display the negative self-image and the deprecating behavior in her stories,

---

[50] (Vega 113-114)

particularly in "El día de los hechos," Vega utilizes a historical setting that allows the silenced voices to be heard. Through a series of flashbacks of the era that forever blemishes the history of the Dominican Republic; a first person narrator tells the story. The story's theme centers on the massacre of Haitians by Dominicans in 1937, during Rafael Trujillo's (1930–1960) dictatorship. The events that compose the story are as follows: an eyewitness, first-person narrator tells the story of Filemón Sagredo el Hijo, who leaves his country, the Dominican Republic, on a rowboat for Puerto Rico, where he establishes a laundromat business. He is visited and killed by a Haitian who came to avenge the betrayal that lead to the killing of his father by Filemón Sagredo el Viejo. The atrocities of the massacre are elaborated, the role of Filemón el Viejo clarified, and Filemón el Hijo killed by the son of the Haitian killed during the massacre.

Ong's characteristic, "close reference to the human lifeworld," gives credence to the accounts of the individual's experience. Since "writing separates the knower from the known and thus sets up conditions for objectivity"[51], personal anecdotes are considered more reliable. Catherine Gallagher and Stephen Greenblatt in *Practicing New*

---

[51] (Ong 46)

Historicism (2000), agree that:

> the desired anecdotes would not, as in the old historicism, epitomize epochal truths, but would instead undermine them. The anecdotes would open history, or place it askew, so that literary texts could find new points of insertion. [52]

The first person narrator confirms testimony by declaring "sí señores, yo estuve allí aquel día a las tres en punto de la tarde"[53]. Contrary to "a written text [that] is basically unresponsive,"[54] credibility of the first–person narrator increases, because she attests to the events; therefore, the subjective narrator's accounts are praiseworthy.[55] Throughout the story, she reiterates her testimony claiming, "pues, sí, señores, yo estaba allí, de cuerpo presente y vi...."[56] Later, talking directly to her readers, she emphatically states: "y no vayan a creer que aquello fue cuestión...."[57] She manipulates the reader's

---

[52] (Gallagher and Greenblatt 51)

[53] (Vega 23)

[54] (Ong 79)

[55] We know that the narrator is a woman because she says "esta servidora podría contarles con lujo de detalles todo lo que sucedió hace tanti cuanto años..." (Vega 23). The emphasis is mine.

[56] (Vega 24)

[57] "y no vayan a creer que aquello fue cuestión...." (Vega 25)

attention by warning him/her against any preconceived ideas about anything other than her story. Intentionally, she draws the reader closer to the details relayed. Clearly, Vega understands that:

> the greater the personalization of this "I" who is regaling us and the more intimate our contact with him on such an armchair-to-sofa level, the greater is this tendency to grant him such credibility in human terms. The less the personalization and the more anonymous and disembodied our host becomes, the weaker grows human contact; such a narrator must then draw his authority solely from the sheer range and depth of his knowledge about the events he narrates....[58]

At the end of the story she confirms her testimony by asserting "para cualquier novedad pueden contar conmigo. Yo lo sé casimente todo. Siempre ando por ahí el día de los hechos"[59]. Disclosing the narrator's closeness to the events emphasizes eyewitness testimony. The immediacy of narrator and events procures fidelity and allegiance, essential elements needed to convince an audience.

---

[58] (Riggan 19)

[59] (Vega 27)

The massacre of Haitians took place at the western border town of Dajabón. By the 1930's, a large Haitian community lived in the Dominican Republic. One group comprised seasonal agricultural workers for the sugarcane plantations; another included families of workers who were "Dominican by birth, but culturally and ethnically Haitian"[60]. The main factor for disliking Haitians was Trujillo's form of nationalism, which praised, emphasized, and encouraged "Hispanidad" or Peninsular Spanish culture.[61] Unsurprisingly, Trujillo disdained and dehumanized all African derived culture. On the western side of the country, Dominican nationalism was not as

---

[60] (Roorda 129)

[61] David Nicholls writes that "Haitian independence [1804] presented a radical challenge to colonialism, to slavery and to the associated ideology of white racialism (...) the very basis of the Haitian claim to independence was racial identity" (Nicholls 3). He suggests that Haitian nationalism was fundamentally rooted in African identity, while across the border; the Spanish colonialist ruled the Dominican Republic. Nicholls states: "although anti-Haitianism (...) had a strong racial content the Dominicans had little conception of peculiar ethnic factors which united themselves. They were part of Hispanic America (...) the Dominican Republic was founded on the idea of el cosmopolitismo in contrast to the Haitian basis of el exclusivismo de una raza (...) The willingness of Dominicans to return to the Spanish empire in 1861... suggests that the centripetal tendencies were much weaker in the Dominican Republic" (Nicholls 13-14).

pronounced as on the eastern side. The Haitian Creole language and African voodoo practices created a climate that preferred a Haitian-Dominican Black culture and not Spanish culture promoted by Trujillo.[62] Fanon argues that Trujillo's form of nationalism resulted from colonial domination.[63]

Believing this, "Trujillo's frontier policy was to change the racial and cultural composition of the area to resemble the self-consciously Hispanic population farther east"[64]. Vega refers to the incident in the story as follows: "el benefactor había proclamado la muerte haitiana a todo lo largo del Masacre. La dominicanización de la frontera estaba en marcha." [65]

"La dominicanización" indicates the racist "Law for

---

[62] After Haiti won her independence from France the Creole language became the national language. Joan Dayan says, "the African born former slaves, who spoke one of at least two or three African languages were silenced and subjugated to the Creole linguistic monopoly..." (Dayan 5).

[63] The effect consciously sought by colonialism was to drive into natives' heads the idea that if the settlers were to leave, they would at once fall back into barbarism, degradation, and bestiality. (Fanon 211)

[64] (Roorda 12)

[65] (Vega 25)

the Dominicanization of Labor" of 1936 designed to drive Haitians and other black West Indians from the Dominican Republic. This law forced many Haitians into exile, even though many were Dominican by birth but could not produce papers establishing birthrights. In the story:

> "algunos habían nacido de este lado de la frontera, críos de haitianos emigrado con dominicano. Pero a la hora del golpe no se le preguntaba a nadie por su mai."[66]

Zielina claims that a new nationalism arises from colonialism. [67]

Haitians were rounded up and slaughtered by the military, which used machetes giving the appearance that the killings were a result of skirmishes among civilians. Freire explains that this behavior originated in colonialism, and he remarks that:

---

[66] (Vega 25)

[67] Este nuevo nacionalismo, por estar asociado a las relaciones socio-económicas y a las sociales, y por el espectro del color que las sigue condimentando, trae también en parte la discriminación. Por estas razones los haitianos, por ejemplo en Cuba, Santo Domingo, Puerto Rico, y los jamaicanos en Panamá y Costa Rica, sufren discriminación en estos países. A pesar de nacer o haber nacido en estos países han sido y son discriminados por su color.... (23)

the oppressed cannot perceive clearly the "order" which serves the interest of the oppressor whose image they have internalized [. . .] they often manifest a type of horizontal violence, striking out at their own comrades.... [68]

Up to twenty thousand were killed because of racial discrimination, according to Dominican Marcio Veloz Maggiolo, "si consideramos que en 1937 casi la mitad de esta población fue exterminada por orden de Trujillo en sólo cuatro o cinco días,... Trujillo actuó movido por un profundo sentido racista...."[69]

The narrator relays this idea as "ya no había en que cargar los muertos. Dondequiera había carretas jartas de cadáveres y bandas de persiguidores borrachos azuzados por el olor a sangre de madamo."[70] The image of the deaths reflects the numerous Haitians persecuted and brutally killed. The reference to "madamo" (a pejorative term used for Haitians adverts to practices of voodoo) punctuates the disdainful sentiments of Dominicans toward Haitians. In essence, profoundly submerged in oppression, the oppressed lacks any consciousness of oppression or his/her disgraceful

---

[68] (Fanon 48)

[69] (Veloz Maggiolo 108)

[70] (Vega 25)

condition or actions. Following the code of conduct already established by oppressors, the oppressed assimilates their abject behavior, inclusively executing it with more violence and intensity. In the story, Vega assumes the task of addressing the people to expose this behavior.

Avoiding the perpetuation of such behavior and the incomplete, negative self–image entails stripping the surface to bring the truth to light, and removing awnings that cover authenticity. Vega supplies the reader with a mirror that compels him/her to reflect and recognize flaws and conflicts that linger in modern day society, flaws that date back generations, for example, "... descendientes de tantos Filemones matados y matones (...) [y] por tantos felicienes matones y matados."[71] As if balancing the responsibility of these two nations, the narrator speaks from a neutral corner, Puerto Rico, and blames both for lack of comradeship.

With focus of the story on the Haitian massacre, Vega makes clear that historical occurrences play a major role in behavioral patterns of people sharing the same island. Neither the historical actions of Haitians nor racial discrimination of Dominicans justifies the behavior of the people. They equally share the responsibility of reflection for

---

[71] (Vega 27)

the purpose of correcting these flaws.

Allen Carey-Webb in Making Subjects: Literature And Emergence Of National Identity (1998), states that:

> a postmodern conception of audience furthers the sense in which postcolonial writing need not always be read exclusively as 'writing back to empire' but as an active engagement in cultural and political discussion with the so-called 'margins.' [72]

By addressing the "so-called margins," Vega makes a plea for the restoration of humanity, through the extraction of the oppressor image, to be replaced with a new one based on a humanity that longs for liberation. Most importantly, this liberation begins with the individual. He/she must recognize the situation, discard the negative oppressor influences, and attempt solidarity among oppressed people. As Freire states, "men must first critically recognize its causes, so that through transforming action they can create a new situation, on which makes possible the pursuit of a fuller humanity" [73].

---

[72] (Carey-Webb 179)

[73] (Freire 32)

IV. Theoretical Characteristics as a Discursive Strategy

Minimizing the gap between text and reader allows a malleable reader greater potential to enter the world of the text. To gain confidence of the "so called margins" (Carey-Webb 179), the distance between text and reader must be reduced. Reduced distance increases the likelihood of persuading the reader to participate. Wolfgang Iser in *Prospecting From Reader Response to Literary Anthropology* (1989), insists that:

> a text that lays things out before the reader in such a way that he can either accept or reject them will lessen the degree of participation, as it allows him nothing but a yes or no... for it is only when the reader is given the chance to participate actively that he will regard the text, whose intention he himself has helped to compose, as real. For we generally tend to regard things that we have made ourselves as being real. [74]

Vega appeals to the idiosyncrasies that characterize the community in order to persuade it "to participate actively." She pursues this end by employing "old formulas

---

[74] (Iser 6)

and themes"[75] to interact with new and often complicated political situations. In doing so, she combines Biblical themes with historical/political occurrences. For example, the epigraph chosen "y Caín mató a Abel, y Abel mató a Caín (23) in "El día de los hechos" is a variation of a common theme used to entice her audience.

Vega insinuates her way into the reader's interest by reacquainting him/her with issues that are familiar and of significance. George Szanto in Narrative Taste and Social Perspectives (1987), notes that:

> an explorative narrative is one which presents new ways of understanding recognizable or previously invisible psychological and social phenomena as these interact and change themselves and each other.[76]

The irony evoked by the epigraph demands the reader's complicity and reflects the existing animosity between nations that share the same island, Haiti and the Dominican Republic.[77] The emphasis on biblical quotations,

---

[75] (Vega 42)

[76] (Szanto 139)

[77] According to Carmen Vázquez Arce, "la ironía exige un lector cómplice, un colaborador inteligente situado en el presente que pueda, mediante el conocimiento de los componentes textuales y extratextuales,

religion, or proverbs complies with Ong's theory because of familiarity. The biblical reference appeals to the reader at once and makes for a more acceptable and empathetic audience. The writer, the narrator, or the eyewitness gets closer to the reader by appealing to communal familiarities.

The story concludes as follows, el mayor de sus dos hijos miraba fijamente sobre las cabezas por donde se había escurrido, en un Chevrolet negro, el pasado de su pasado de su padre"[78]. This echoes the Old Testament's refrain "visiting the iniquity of the fathers upon the children, and upon the children's children unto the third and to the fourth generation" (Ex. 20.5). The biblical quote and conclusion of the story exemplifies the tactics of "conservative and

---

descodifican el verdadero significado de las palabras" (293). Arce suggests that there are two levels of understanding in the works of Puerto Rican writers Luis Rafael Sánchez and Félix Córdova Iturregui. The first level is a disguise that only allows the surface to be revealed. That is, if the reader is astute, complicity will be established and the reader will move into the second level. If not he will remain in the first level, which is the ideological level. However, the second level is considered advanced because it entails complicity and deciphering the irony that prevails in the story. She adds, "la ironía constituye una estrategia crítica fundamental para examinar, desmontar, desarticular y burlarse en sus narraciones de la situación colonial que rige la vida de los puertorriqueños". (Arce 193)

[78] (Vega 27)

traditionalist" narrative. This characteristic:

> lodges… in managing a particular interaction with this
> audience (...) at every telling the story has to be
> introduced uniquely into a unique situation, for in oral
> cultures an audience must be brought to respond,
> often vigorously. [79]

The ability of the "conservative and traditionalist" narrator to mix, repeat, and combine familiar expressions wins over acceptance of the audience. Writers may "introduce new elements into old stories similarly new stories may be introduced with old elements."[80]; .[81] Vega captivates the reader by presenting themes of relevance to him/her with for the purpose of producing a vicarious experience through the lived or relived the events. For instance, in the story, the narrator tells us how:

> …Filemón Sagredo el Viejo no acababa de decidirse a
> denunciar al haitiano … Pero cuando Felicién pidió
> refugio, lo pensó dos veces para al fin murmurar un
> sícagado de indecisión. El recuerdo de su padre
> muerto en Haiti durante la ocupación yanquí era una

---

[79] (Ong 42)

[80] (Ong 42)

[81] Ong notes that "old formulas and themes" may be scrambled and repeated as often as possible while maintaining some originality.

espina en pleno galillo. Lo habían ahorcado los cacos de Péralte, colgándolo del asta de una bandera gringa por espía y delator. Injustamente, por cierto. Lo confundieron con otro dominicano....[82]

The allusion is to the invasion of Haiti by the United States in 1915. Although, the invasion was met with minimal resistance, Charlemagne Péralte and Benoit Batraville led the Cacos rebellion in 1918 to expel the northern invaders from their homeland. Betrayal of Péralte by a family member eventually led to his death and the Cacos rebellion was put down. The central theme of brother killing brother in the story is highlighted, and Vega embellishes the story with relevant historical themes that stress the central theme for the purpose of acknowledging them. By venturing into a familiar theme (Cain and Abel and the massacre of Haitians by Dominicans) with political, historical, and social implications, Vega reduces the distance between text and reader. As Iser claims:

> meanings in literary texts are generated in the act of reading;... when reading the words of past ages,... we are actually transported back into those times and move in historical circumstances as if we belonged to them or as the past were again the present... It is we

---

[82] . (Vega 26)

who bring the text to life... however far back in the past it may lie, comes alive in the present. [83]

By juxtaposing the written account and testimony of an eyewitness, Vega provides an alternative to the official account with enormous importance placed on the reevaluation of the historical perspective recounted. "By remembering the past, these authors endeavor to shape a future less marked by the hardships that have plagued them"[84]. Vega's constant questioning of written history and the narrating of the regions' histories and stories, based on the experiences of the people possesses cathartic and healing powers.

V. Traces of Santería in "Encancaranublado"

Some minority writers who wish to remain loyal to and within the realms of their culture do so through experimentation. To accomplish this they extract cultural elements that bind reader to text while deviating from the dominant order criteria because:

---

[83] (Iser 5)

[84] (Cohn 190)

... minority discourse... claims that the languages of power and the historical assumptions and distortions they have engendered endow their users, potentially at least, with a power-based vision of the world and with a consciousness of the world that tends to devalue those who are different and less powerful... minority literature is not just jettisoned against the dominant canon and its hegemonic centers, but also is immersed in those substratum African/African-American linguistic forms customarily thought to be outside the possibilities of creativity.[85]

These writers aspire to attract attention of native people through what Norman Holland, in *Readers Reading* (1975), refers to as "identity themes"[86]. Morsels of culture are dispersed throughout the story for the reader to decipher, identify, and enjoy. Deleuze and Guattari believe that language should be thrust to the limit; such language experimentation is particularly crucial for minorities who want to remain minorities and affirms perspectives (in their works) reflective of their cultural spheres; manifested "in connection with a specific cultural context"[87].

---

[85] (Kubayanda 118)

[86] (Holland 111)

[87] (Deleuze and Guattari 14)

Zielina corroborates this idea and insists that its efficaciousness depends on the "lector informado" familiar with "africanía." The "lector" must be "un lector entrenado en las cosas del Caribe, capaz de seguir ciertas pistas ofrecidas a través de la transculturación, de la idea del nacionalismo y sincretismo que aparecen en el texto."[88]For this reason the African cultural vestiges in the story "Encancaranublado" are unquestionable to the reader of "africanía." The "masters of these codes"[89] decode the suggestions and tinges of Santería extant throughout the story.

The events of the story are as follows. A Haitian sails a small boat en route to Miami with hopes of escaping poverty in his homeland. Along the way he picks up a Dominican and later a Cuban who have capsized at sea. Essentially, all have left their countries in order to flee economic deprivation and political uncertainties. Although they come from different countries, they are all "antillano, negro, y pobre"[90] and dream of the "pursuit of happiness"[91] in the United States.

---

[88] (Zielina 31)

[89] (Zielima 15)

[90] (Zielima 14)

[91] (Zielima 13)

This is suggested in the title of the story "Encancaranublado" and the epigraph:

El cielo está encancaranublado.quién lo encancaranublaría? El que lo encancaranubló buen encancaranublador sería.[92]

The epigraph may be an invocation from these men who blindly and dangerously float around in the Caribbean Sea. It also, for the reader of "africanía," evokes the spirits of Orishas, Obatalá and Changó, two Orishas who have dwellings in the sky and clouds and possess power over the natural elements. Their attributes, characteristics, and powers appear throughout the story.

Reverberations of the nebulous and ambiguous situation faced by the men reflect the skepticism that abounds in the story. The narrator makes clear the haphazard future. Nevertheless, hope dwells in the heart of the reader of "africanía" as well as the men. The familiarity with and faith in Santería does not allow despair to creep in. Zielina claims that "el lector de la "africanía" tiene que llenar "huecos," (...) tiene que suplir, con su experiencia de cultura sincrética ...."[93] Hence, the reader of "africanía" easily

---

[92] (Zielima 13)

[93] (Zielima 32)

unravels the symbolism. For example, the beginning of the story is as follows:

> septiembre, agitador profesional de huracanes, avisa guerra llenando los mares de erizos y aguavivas. Un vientecito sospechoso hincha la guayabera que funge de vela en la improvisada embarcación. El cielo es una conga encojonada para bembé de potencias.[94]

The month of September alludes to hues of Obatalá's skills. Obatalá, according to legend, was born in September and endowed with the kingdom of earth by the creator Olorún-Olofi. When one invokes his powers he can safely provide guidance to the desired destination, in this case, Miami.[95] The danger of the journey escalates in September because of the hurricanes that afflict that area during this season. As the ninth month of the year, September symbolizes the birth of something new or starting over for these men seeking a better life in the United States, "ese país de progreso."[96]

---

[94] (Zielima 13)

[95] Obatalá, syncretized as Our Lady of Lourdes, in an outrage of jealousy yanks out his wife's eyes leaving her blind. Subsequently, he is endowed with the capacity of guidance and clarity. (González-Whippler)

[96] (Zielima 17)

However, a shadow of doubt looms over their future, when the American ship rescues them, after capsizing at sea. The crude reality of "aquí si quieren comer tienen que meter mano y duro. Estos gringos no les dan na gratis ni a su mai"[97], brings to mind Deleuze and Guattari's idea that "minority literature" is always attached to the political. They assert that:

> literature finds itself positively charged with the role and function of collective, and even revolutionary, enunciation. It is literature that produces an active solidarity in spite of skepticism; and if the writer is in the margins or completely outside his or her fragile community, this situation allows the writer all the more the possibility to express another possible community and to forge the means for another consciousness and another sensibility....[98]

The men in the story, after consuming their provisions of "casabe, ...mazorcas de maíz, tabaco y ron..."[99], resume their hopes and quest for a better life. "Almorzados el casabe y las mazorcas, los compinches reaunudaron su análisis socioeconómico [. . .] con la contentura del que liga los encantos de la Estatua de la Libertad bajo la desgastada

---

[97] (Zielima 20)

[98] (Deleuze and Guattari 17)

[99] (Zielima 16)

tunica."[100] The image of the Statue of Liberty with the "wasted tunic" touches the political issue, which Deleuze and Guattari insist is forever present in "minority literature." It blatantly nullifies the dreams of the men's "pursuit of happiness." Iris Zavala in Colonialism and Culture (1992), adds that [101]

The provisions serve as an offering to Changó for the purpose of keeping him happy, prepared, and adept to perform his craft. That is: [102]

Changó, the son of Kalunga, the Orisha of the water, inherently rules and dominates the water. During tempestuous times his powers are elicited, for example (González–Whippler 118)[103] The three men in the story, Antenor, Diógenes, and Carmelo, supplicate his mercy and power when their boat capsizes. The immersion in water

---

[100] (Zielima 17)

[101] the notion of ideologeme suggests the possibility of relating images, experiences, and discourse allows us to abandon the traditional thematic concept and to capture content from an ideological perspective which is part of class struggle. Each narrative, or each thematic construct incorporates new meanings as it is recontextualized. (14)

[102] luego que Changó comió y bebió a su entera satisfacción, vuelve su atención a los presentes, quienes le piden entonces consejos respecto a sus problemas y lo interrogan en relación con sus negocios urgentes. (63)

[103] "del relámpago y del rayo, nada podía ser más natural que invocarlo cuando hay una severa tempestad eléctrica."

signifies death and annihilation on the one hand, but rebirth and regeneration on the other, since immersion intensifies the life force (Cirlot 365). The narration is as follows: [104]

While the forces of "Altagracia, la Caridad del Cobre y las Siete Potencias Africanas" rescue them from the perils of the elements, who will save them from the racism to which they will be subjected?[105] Once on the ship, the captain takes a look at them and shouts
–get those niggers down there and let the spiks take care of 'em [. . .] compartieron su primera mirada post naufragio: mixta de alivio y de susto sofrita en esperanzas ligeramente sancochadas. Minutos después [. . .] tuvieron la grata experiencia de escuchar su lengua materna, algo maltratada pero siempre reconocible. (20)

As hopes of their dreams evaporate, they realize that

---

[104] y a pique se fueron.... A pique y lloviendo, con truenos y viento... -- !Un barco!, gritó Carmelo.... Las tres voces náufragas se unieron en un largo, agudo y optimista alarido de auxilio. Y al cabo de un rato --y no me pregunten cómo el carajo se zapatearon a los tiburones porque fue sin duda un milagro conjunto de la Altagracia, la Caridad del Cobre y las Siete Potencias Africanas-- los habían rescatado.... (19)

[105] La Virgen de Altagracia is the patron saint of the Dominican Republic, La Virgen de la Caridad del Cobre is the patron saint of Cuba and Las Siete Potencias represent the voodoo practices of Haiti.

in spite of differences or (Zielina 165)[106] they will continue to be (14)[107] Befittingly, the story ends with the image of (20), a metaphor for the laborious prospects awaiting them, since they have been advised (20)[108] At the beginning of the story the "brazo" serves another function. (13)[109] indicates the obstruction to reaching their destination. However, at the end of the story, ironically, "un brazo negro" belonging to a Puerto Rican who speaks the language "algo maltratada" becomes the link between their Caribbean culture and the North American culture, which they will have to assimilate. This commingling of cultures in actuality reveals itself as the clash of cultures unequivocably adumbrated by Nicolás Guillén in the following poem "Canción puertorriqueña":[110]

---

[106] "pedacitos de cultura, de idioma, de ideologías, de creencias"

[107] "antillano, negro, y pobre."

[108] "si quieren comer tienen que meter mano...."

[109] "Ese mollerudo brazo de mar que lo separa del pursuit of happiness"

[110] ¿Cómo estás, Puerto Rico,

tú de socio asociado en sociedad?

Al pie de cocoteros y guitarras,

bajo la luna y junto al mar,

qué suave honor andar del brazo,

brazo con brazo, del Tío Sam!

¿En que lengua me entiendes,

en qué lengua por fin te podré hablar,

si en yes,

si en sí,

Furthermore, according to Yoruba legend, man was created without a head "la cual fue añadida por Obatalá." (110)[111] Various parts of the body "brazo, cara, ojos, cabeza, mano," mentioned in the story serve to elicit the image of a new creation. According to santería belief (110)[112], hence, he shapes (in this case reshapes) the fragmented human body and spirit with a new sense of consciousness. Luis Garalzaga confirms that [113]

Vega appeals to the idiosyncrasies that embody that community. She assumes responsibility of connecting the reader to text. For instance, she attracts the reader's attention through "identity themes" (Holland 111). In the

---

si en bien,

si en well,

si en mal,

si en bad, si en very bad?.... (31)

[111] "la cual fue añadida por Obatalá."

[112] "toda la estructura ósea del cuerpo pertenece a Obatalá (...) y también la cabeza y los sesos"

[113] es la necesidad de que nuestra desgarrada conciencia colectiva,... se amplifique y se abra a esa "otredad", asumiendo y recuperando los fragmentos de la historia espiritual del hombre que han quedado plasmados y condensados en los símbolos. Dichos símbolos comparecen así como documento dotados de una dignidad humana y de una significación filosófica, que son capaces de revelar ciertas dimensiones de la vida humana olvidadas o desfiguradas en las sociedades modernas. (18)

stories "El día de los hechos" and "Encancaranublado," she intends to create another perspectiive of history and identity for the people. That is, the themes of history, racism, and Santería addressed in these stories are not unfamiliar to the readers of "africanía." [114]

By addressing these issues she offers another perspective from which to view their reality. Understanding how the negative self-image impedes development of a national consciousness, she offers a mirror to the reader by probing issues of identity and national culture. She exposes misconceptions and distortions rooted in colonialism through what Thadious Davis refers to (9)[115].

---

[114] Vega... ilustra[] cómo la escritura histórica depende de autores que dibujan un cuadro ideológicamente interesado de la historia. En Vega la historia presupone una lucha entre la versión oficial y las versiones silenciadadas de los eventos históricos. Es rasgo evidentísimo que ... explícitamente contextualiza la[] ideología[] no como manifestación de un discurso totalizante, eterno y natural sino segun la especificidad histórica que produce esa[] ideología. (Cruz 65)

[115] "as the self-consciously reconfiguring history and identity through the inversion of traditional power structures..."

VI. The language in "El día de los hechos" and "Encancaranublado"

To continue along the path of deterritorialization, Vega resorts to what Vicente Francisco Torres en La novela bolero latinoamericana (1998) refers to as (184)[116] which reflects reality and the experiences of the common people. The language permeates the story with (Vega 314)[117], an idea, which favors "parodia sacra", elaborated Mikhail M. Bakhtin in The Dialogic Imagination (1981). [118]

---

[116] "el lenguaje danzarín, musical y juguetón [que] aparece asociado al mundo del trópico y de los negros alegres y querendones..."

[117] "los juegos de palabras [que] nos permiten echar mano de la cultura..."

[118] It is an intentional dialogized hybrid, but a hybrid of different languages. It is a dialogue between languages, although one of them (the vulgar) is present only as an actively dialogizing backdrop. What we have is never-ending folkloric dialogic: the dispute between a dismal sacred word and a cheerful folk word.... Another's sacred word, uttered in a foreign language, is degraded by the accents of vulgar folk languages, re-evaluated and reinterpreted against the backdrop of these languages, and congeals to the point where it becomes a ridiculous image, the comic carnival mask of a narrow and joyless pedant, and unctious hypocritical old bigot, a stingy and dried up miser. This manuscript tradition of "parodia sacra," prodigious in scope and almost a thousand years long, is a remarkable and as yet poorly used document testifying to an intense struggle and interanimation among languages. A struggle that occurred everywhere in Western Europe. This was a language drama

This "never-ending folkloric dialogic" attracts the participation of the Caribbean reader. The integration of the reader in the story facilitates the connection and the identification with the text. The text appeals to the idiosyncrasies of popular culture, and this literature requires a more careful and thorough research of the reading for one not familiar with that culture.

As Deleuze and Guattari have suggested, such a language becomes a form of deterritorialization because:
These "linguistic Third World zones" provide a sense of identity for the reader, as manifested in the stories. For instance, the focus becomes the North American, with an indigenous flavor. In "El día de los hechos" the narrator, presumably a Dominican living in Puerto Rico, describes the incidents that lead to the killing of Haitian, Felicién, by comparing the temperature of that day to the heat expelled from Filemón's laundromat. She narrates as follows: "... yo estuve allí aquel día a las tres en punto de la tarde cuando la calor de afuera era piragua al lado del infierno que jervía en aquel laundry."[119] (23)[120] The reference to identification

---

played out as if it were a gay farce. It was linguistic Saturnalia--lingua sacra pileata. (76-77)

[119] a language is open to an extensive utilization that makes it take flight along creative lines of escape which, no matter how slowly, no matter how cautiously can now form an absolute deterritorialization.... To

"piragua" gives the reader something to relate to from the start of the story.

Later she captures the attention of the reader (particularly the Dominican) with cultural tidbits and indigenous entities that decorate the text, which makes for a more delectable reading environment, for instance, [121]

Such Dominican qualities as foods, "sancocho y el morir soñando," geographical location, "el Cibao", music, "un merengue ripiao" and the Dominican accent, "un hablaicito particulai" accentuate the sense of familiarity,[122]

---

make use of the polylingualism of one's own language, to make a mirror or intensive use of it, to oppose the oppressed quality of this language to its oppressive quality, to find points of nonculture or underdevelopment, linguistic Third World zones by which a language can escape.... (26–27)

[120] A piragua is a "snow-cone" like refreshing dessert made of crushed ice and flavored with a syrup made of tropical fruit such as mangos, tamarinds, or coconut.

[121] ... entre kioscos y pensiones dominicanas, corrían el sancocho y el morir soñando talmente como en el Cibao. Si a ratos pellizcaba la nostalgia de un merengue ripiao y de un hablaicito paiticulai, siempre se podía dar un brinquito a la República pa cumplir con los viejos y echar su figureo en la plaza.... (23)

[122] Sancocho is a stew like soup made of roots native to the Caribbean or tropical climate. Morir soñando is a refreshing drink made of orange juice, milk, spices and ice made exclusively in the Dominican Republic.

and help retain the attention of the reader. Vega vigorously and faithfully appeals to Dominican cultural moorings. Stephen Greenblatt in "Culture" (1990), states that: [123]

Vega illustrates her "master[y] of these codes" well manifested in "el lenguaje festivo" which reflects gaity and cheerfulness that encompasses the soul of the people no matter the situation. However, in the story "Encancaranublado" the brusque, vulgar, and condescending language employed disparages and taunts the Spanish-speaking Caribbean people. For instance, reference to Haiti's illiteracy, (17)[124], and the mention of different shades

---

The idea of food and drink brings to mind Francois Rabelais since, "he does affirm the lofty importance of eating and drinking in human life, and strives to justify them ideologically, to make them respectable, to erect a culture for them" (Bakhtin 185). Vega is trying to erect a culture for Caribbean cuisine by lauding all that is Caribbean that perhaps has been overlooked.

[123] anthropologists are centrally concerned with a culture's kinship system -- its conception of family relationships [. . .] and with its narratives -- myths, folktales, and sacred stories. The two concerns are linked, for a culture's narratives, like its kinship arrangements, are crucial indices of the prevailing codes governing human mobility and constraint. Great writers are precisely masters of these codes, specialists in cultural exchange. (230)

[124] "de algo tenía que servir el record de analfabetismo mundial que nadie le disputaba a su país"

of complexion, racial categories and classifications, belittle and ridicule blacks. The words and phrases such as, (15)[125], which means "kinky hair", and "prieto" which although may be a term of endearment, may also be a pejorative term used for blacks, and "jincho," a term used for a high yellow black person in the Spanish-speaking Caribbean islands, may easily be misunderstood by non-natives.

Although the language clings to a festive sentiment, the episodes described may not be as pleasurable. For instance, in "El día de los hechos" the semblance of ferocity negates the gaity of the language. The narrator describes a macabre incident (the killing of Filemón el abuelo by Haitians) as follows: [126]

The violent language describing the hanging of Filemón el abuelo by Péralte's Cacos contrasts the festive language affecting a polarity. The juxtaposition of this antithesis provides an image of a violent act executed with a musical backdrop. It elicits the image of Filemón swinging or swaying as if "bailando su dernier carabiné en el aire

---

[125] "cabeza encrespada"

[126] lo habían ahorcado los cacos de Péralte, colgándolo del asta de una bandera gringa por espía y delator... Esto para mí es bolero viejo. Yo alcancé a ver los pies de Filemón abuelo bailando su dernier carabiné en el aire haitiano. (26)

haitiano." The idea of "los pies... en el aire haitiano" parallels the image of Filemón "colgando del asta." The double image evoked, one of a lynching, the other of a party, while it documents an injustice it captures the festive spirit, an intricate part of Caribbean popular culture. Therefore, it is not unusual for the narrator to remark "esto para mi es bolero viejo." Torres claims that: [127]

The theme of brother killing brother senselessly, conveyed in the epigraph "Y Abel mató a Caín y Caín mató a Abel" matches that of the song "El negro bembón."[128] Amidst all the Filemones and Felicienes "matones y matados," at some point the reader becomes confused and completely uncertain of whom the Haitian or the Dominican might be. Vega intentionally creates this atmosphere of confusion in order to underline the disparity that exists among people who share the same background. The lyrics of the song

---

[127] el bolero (...) no permitía un desarrollo anecdótico tan completo como el del tango. Por esto muestra un estado del corazón.... En este palimpsesto el bolero implora (...) habla de la ruptura, el abandono, el desengaño y la ansiedad; reprocha, amenaza, muestra resentimiento, rencor o nostalgia (...) renuncia, se conforma, asume la ausencia o la traición y perdona, injuria y hasta agradece. (82)

[128] Bembón is the word used in the Spanish-speaking Caribbean for a person with big lips. It is usually used in a condescending manner, but it may also be used jokingly.

highlight and document the themes of brother killing brother and racial injustice. [129]

The negative self–image and disgraceful behavior born of colonialism evident in the song compares to aspects of Caribbean life, this self–hate manifested in the song is ridiculed with a sense of humor. Vega says: [130]

---

[129] Mataron al negro bembón

mataron al negro bembón

hoy se llora noche y día

porque al negrito bembón todo el mundo lo quería

porque al negrito bembón todo el mundo lo quería

y llegó la policía y arrestaron al matón

uno de los policías él también era bembón

le tocó la mala suerte de hacer la investigación

le tocó la mala suerte de hacer la investigación

sabe la pregunta que le hizo al matón

porque lo mató diga usted la razón

sabe la respuesta que le dio el matón

yo lo maté por ser tan bembón

el guardia escondio la bemba y le dijo

eso no es razón, para matar al bembón....

[130] el humor está presente en esta literatura caribeñista como rasgo cultural que también se halla muy presente en nuestra musica popular. Es además una manera de enganchar al lector, de hacerle pasar cosas terribles, o muy dolorosas, pero dándole la pildora, aunque a veces, el humor es agresivo, zahiriente, irónico, desacralizante. (314 Torres)

Bakhtin also asserts that: [131]

The sentiments of the song equal those of the story. Vega insists that, "la música puertorriqueña siempre ha sido la gran adelantada del país... Como la música ha roto barreras, la literatura se ha agarrado de esa fuerza para salir." (314) In the song, in addition to observing the source of Vega's inspiration -- everyday life -- we observe the role of the "contre-partie," which plays a reversed role played with the intention of parodying; he is considered a double. According to Bakhtin, "everything serious had to have, and indeed did have, its comic double. As in Saturnalia the clown was the double of the ruler and the slave the double of the master" (58). The policeman in the song plays role of the double of "el negro bembón." He investigates the crime and asks the killer, ¿por qué lo mató? After hearing the response of the killer, "yo lo maté por ser tan bembón," the policeman, realizing the possibility of becoming another victim of racial prejudice, "escondio la bemba y le dijo, eso

---

[131] Laughter proved to be just as profoundly productive and deathless a creation of Rome as Roman Law. This laughter broke through the grim atmosphere of seriousness of the Middle Ages to fertilize the great creations of Renaissance literature; up to this day it continues to resonate in [. . .] literature. (58)

no es razón." This idea coincides with [132]

Hence, musicality in the works of Vega, in addition to appealing to the musical sense of the people, an inherent part of the culture, seizes the attention of the native reader, because Vega claims that:[133]

According to her, these elements are important factors of Caribbean culture that play a major role in literature. Therefore, musicality characteristic of the Caribbean spirit filled with percussion and rhythm-loaded

---

[132] the literary and artistic consciousness of the Roman [who] could not imagine [that] a serious form was perceived as only fragment, only half a whole; the fullness of the whole was achieved only upon adding the comic contre-partie of this form. (Bakhtin 58)

[133] Puede que nuestra literatura no se conozca mucho en el extranjero, pero nuestra música sí, hasta en los sitios más inesperados.... la literatura siempre gira en torno a esa obsesión de la nacionalidad como no se construye en la política, tratamos de construirla en la literatura. Y el uso del lenguaje específico es una manera de construirla. Los juego de palabras nos permiten echar mano de la cultura popular. Esta generación de escritores [. . .] los que surgieron de los sesenta--ha echado mano de elementos de la cultura popular muy importantes, entre ellos, la música, el humor, el baile, el lenguaje festivo, la santería, el espiritismo; todo lo popular ha sido aprovechado para decir el país.... Estos elementos son tan importantes, son experiencias tan vigentes y auténticas que nos hemos sentido integrados a ellos, como partícipes más que observadores. (34)

tunes standout in the story "Encancaranublado."

The multitude of alliterations enclosed in the story at times gives the sensation that one is either dancing or singing a happy rhythmic song. For example, "otro pasajero, otra alma, otro estómago" (15), "pica caña y caña pica"(16) and "caridad contra caridad no es caridad." (16) The hard sound of the stopped, voiceless consonants such as the letters t and c reverberate throughout the text, and the multiple syllables imitate the musical instruments native to the Caribbean islands.[134] This exemplifies the concept of "deterritorialization" because its usage "takes flight along creative lines of escape" (26).

Although comprehensible and engaging to the reader of "africanía," this particularity may be impenetrable to the reader not familiar with the culture, because the language seeks to escape colonial language. [135]

---

[134] Some of these instruments include the clave (two sticks struck against each other producing sounds and the most basic that keeps the music together (in salsa music) such as tac, tac, tac, tac tac. Other instruments include various drums (timbales, congas, bongos) and the cowbell.

[135] It is only from that moment that we can speak of a national literature. Here there is, at the level of literary creation, the taking up and clarification of themes which are typically nationalist. This may be properly called a literature of combat, in the sense that it calls on the

In essence, Vega manipulates her literary skills to attract the attention of her audience by appealing to their idiosyncrasies. She penetrates the reality of different aspects of popular culture in the Spanish-speaking Caribbean. Instead of portraying stereotyped characters, she resorts to humanizing the image of blacks by representing various aspects and dimensions of a more credible and genuine black psyche.

---

whole people to fight for their existence as a nation. It is a literature of combat, because it molds the national consciousness, giving it form and contours and flinging open before it new and boundless horizons; it is a literature of combat because it assumes responsibility, and because it is the will to liberty expressed in terms of time and space. (Fanon 240)

Chapter 3
Reconstructing Dominican Identity

Get up, stand up, don't give up the fight!
– Bob Marley [136]

Following this new trend, Blas Jiménez also affirms black identity through positive images that replace negative ones once forged in literature. In his collection of poems Caribe africano en despertar, he insists on relinquishing the negative values established by the colonial system. He is [137]

The poetry concentrates on a positive self-image of blacks and engages in a discourse that attempts to "locate, identify, and legitimize" (Cox 10) the life and position of blacks in the Dominican Republic. It plays a major role in discarding the negative concepts that hamper the possibilities of a suitable and dignified image for blacks.

---

[136] Bob Marley (1945–1981) was a Jamaican singer-songwriter who popularized reggae music, through his fiery and revolutionary lyrics, which preached freedom for blacks around the world.

[137] ...commited to a politics of cultural transformation that would constructively change the lot of the black underclass and thus positively impact the culture as a whole need to make decolonizing our minds and imagination central when we educate for critical consciousness. (Hooks 182)

Caribe africano en despertar is structured in three sections ("libros") entitled, "Caribe," "Africano," and "En despertar," a division which agrees with Hugo Achugar's theory that all the elements that bind a book from the beginning to the end [138]

Each "libro" begins with an epigraph that anticipates and substantiates the theme of that particular section, which consequently adheres and contributes to the overall message of the collection, that is, to rescue the people from a (West 102)[139]. The "walking nihilists" are those individuals who proudly exist without any notion of consciousness; they are (West 102)[140].

In this chapter, we will illustrate how Jiménez, through his text, attempts to correct the stereotypes and racial myths that have informed the psyche of Caribbean people. Jiménez has replaced the negative traditional images

---

[138] … function as elements marked by the socio-historical process and conditions of productions. They are at once tied to the ideological and aesthetic project of the book of poems and socially articulated to its time. (653)

[139] "walking nihilism"

[140] "highly anxiety-ridden, insecure, willing to be co-opted and incorporated into the power that be, concerned with racism to the degree that it poses constraints on upward social mobility"

with positive statements that reconstruct a new self–image for blacks. The chapter is divided into five sections; the first section, "Road to consciousness," will elucidate and define the applicable theory that will serve as the framework for the subsequent textual analysis. Kubayanda claims that the route to consciousness is through the following stages: "stoicism," "skepticism," "unhappy consciousness," and "rational consciousness." The interaction of the four stages is evident in Jiménez's collection of poems.

The second section, "Roots of Negrism," will provide a brief background of this movement. The term "negrism," briefly explained, establishes some of the characteristics that were born of it, as well as, their relation to contemporary black writers. Puerto Rican poet Luis Palés Matos (1891–1959), one of the pioneers of this movement, will be introduced and discussed. Negrism's relevance lies in that [141]

The third section, "History Dominican Style," will draft the historical background of racial discrimination in the

---

[141] negritude poetic discourse [. . .] emerged largely against this backdrop of Caribbean self–review and self–recognition; it served as an intellectual and cultural attempt to affirm a Caribbean affinity with Africa as well as to express faith in the Caribbean person. (Kubayanda 16)

Dominican Republic for the purpose of establishing its roots. It will highlight the poem "Discriminación a la dominicana" for the purpose of substantiating the background information. The fourth section, "A Message of Pride and Resistance," will provide a brief background of the history of resistance as a prelude to the parallel between the dedication of the collection of poems and the poem "Guerrillero." In the fifth section, divided into three parts: "Reconstructing An Identity," "Affirming Identity," and "A New Dawn," we analyze selected poems from Jiménez's collection, and in the poems analyzed we theorize that, in order for blacks to rescue their dignity, they must focus on reexamining and redefining history so that it reflects their reality. Moreover, we emphasize that the role of conscientious contemporary poets aims to restore the nullified dignity of blacks to help escape the "walking nihilism," which Cornel West defines in Prophetic Reflections: Notes on Race and Power in America (1993), as (102)[142].

---

[142] "the imposing of closure on the human organism intentionally, by that organism itself"

I. The Road to Consciousness

The human personality possesses two oppositional forces, one of inferiority, the other of superiority. G.W.F. Hegel affirms, and Kubayanda agrees, that [143]

In order to be free from this bondage, a journey through the various stages is necessary for the purpose of attaining consciousness. Kubanyanda also believes in a series of stages for the attainment of consciousness. The first stage of "stoicism" manifests the resignation of the individual to that particular state. The individual's true sentiments are never known or recognized because he/she remains complacent and settled in a perpetual state of "stoicism." Settled in this state he/she never strives for or achieves anything; instead, the tendency is to play the role of the stupefied, colonized individual. The second stage of "skepticism" allows the individual to question the previous condition. He/she acknowledges self-inculcation, questions it, but does little to extirpate it or bring about a change.

---

[143] central to this theory is a warring process of negation and recognition. Negation involves the refusal of the bondsman to accept his position of weakness and servitude. Recognition entails a belligerent quest for attention or acknowledgement by an Other. Thus fulfillment in bondage or lordship seems impossible without due attention from the Other. (Hegel 37)

Nevertheless, the self–interrogation effects advancement towards consciousness.

The third stage, "unhappy consciousness," illustrates the individual's acknowledgement of his/her own dual existentiality. Discontented and miserable, the individual realizes that he/she plays two roles within the oppressive condition. Playing a subservient role eventually gives rise to a sense of discomfort within the individual that leads to a certain degree of awareness, a progressive movement toward the stage of "unhappy consciousness." The fourth and final stage, "rational consciousness," is the realization of the condition of "unhappy unconscious." However, with an awareness and desire of going forward because "… as he breaks his 'adhesion' and objectifies the reality from which he starts to emerge, he begins to integrate himself as a Subject (an I) confronting an object (reality)." According to Freire, the individual now realizes his/her detachment from self, and when (174)[144], the individual moves toward removing all manacles that bind him/her to the ways of the "other" and progresses toward becoming a human being with a sense of consciousness.

---

[144] "he becomes a true individual"

II. Roots of Negrism

During the early part of the twentieth century, Europeans who visited Africa were impressed with the art of native people and wanted to emulate its style. Cubism was, in part, born out of the interest of geometric shapes that Africans applied to their sculptures. Curiosity concerning black culture became a fad and many artists were attracted to the theme. This attraction was not limited to Europeans; anthropologists such as the Cuban Fernando Ortíz (1881–1969), known for works such as Contrapunteo cubano del tabaco y el azúcar (1947), La africanía de la música folklórica de Cuba (1950), among others, and the Brazilian Raymondo Nina Rodrigues known for O animismo fetichista dos negros bahianos; prefacio e notas de Arthur Ramos (1935), began to publish works that studied the contribution of blacks to culture and society. Also, the works of artists such as Pablo Picasso (1881–1973), Georges Braque (1882–1963), and Juan Gris (1887–1927), among others, are preliminary to the poetic movement of "negrism." This movement has been defined in various ways, and the following two definitions, although different, provide a unique perspective of negrism: [145]

---

[145] a form of poetry characterized by African sounding words, rhythms and language, yet, a shallow understanding of black culture by some

The European artists' interest in the art and culture of African nations spread to Caribbean nations because of their black population. However, the works circulating around the literary world did not depict blacks in a positive light. Instead, the tendency was a caricaturesque portrayal of blacks. Luis Palés Matos is one of the first to include blacks or black themes in his poetry, and according to Margot Arce de Vázquez, "en Hispanoamérica precede a todos los poetas y escritores del negrismo en lengua española [. . .]" (qtd. in Jackson XI). In 1937, he publishes his best-known work, Tuntún de pasa y grifería. Although considered a pioneer of the movement negrismo, Aníbal González has held that his view of black culture was the same as that of the intellectuals of that period. Their main concern was with the mulatto culture and not necessarily the black culture. (González 567) Palés has been criticized for being removed from black

---

white discoverers of the negro is partly responsible for the negative and, at best one dimensional images of blacks widely perpetuated in Spanish American literature. (Jackson 469)

Negritude poetic discourse [. . .] emerged largely against this backdrop of Caribbean self-review and self-recognition; it served as an intellectual and cultural attempt to affirm a Caribbean affinity with Africa as well as to express faith in the Caribbean person [. . .] the idea of Africa and of the Caribbean was articulated in the very European languages for which Africa and the African diaspora had been nothing but a shadow Africa. (Kubayanda 16)

culture; Kubayanda maintains (24)[146]

III. History Dominican Style

Important historical points reveal the Dominican Republic's system of discrimination. Discrimination has a long tradition in the colonial system and its perpetuation has hindered the growth of national identity. The historical synopsis, while it provides background information, converges with the poem "Discriminación a la dominicana," which conveys a historically ironic perspective that protests the social, racial, and economic injustices that Dominicans impose on their own people.

When Columbus arrived on Hispaniola in 1492, he brought with him the medieval social values and traditions of Spain. The expulsion of the Jews and Moors after the conquest of Granada in 1492 did not end the quest for pure blood; in fact, it was intensified and, in the Caribbean, the concept of limpieza de sangre (purity of blood) evolved

---

[146] "this poet, it seems appropriate to add, passionately dreams about a primitive force in the form of an unconscious blackness which fails to harmonize with his conscious ("civilized") self."

drastically. "Skin color became not only quite relevant but it was also converted into an essential determinant. Mixed blood came to be viewed as conclusive evidence of what was described as moral deficiency and intellectual inferiority" (Cambeira 90).

The color-coding system in Latin America and the Caribbean was different from that of the United States, where anyone who had an ounce of black blood was considered black. In the Spanish-speaking Caribbean, the socio-economic status of the people depended on their degree of white blood. This system, which classified people based on their degree of whiteness, was utilized by the hegemonic structures in order to reiterate the idea of white superiority, and gave rise to the concept of black inferiority. Thus, privileges were awarded on the basis of the amount of one's white blood. The poem "Discriminación a la dominicana," ridicules the belief in the color-coding system. The preposterous and farcical desire to be a lighter shade, "tú no eres negro / tú eres un indio," exemplify the ludicrous claim to being Indian, since the Indians were exterminated during the early stages of the colonial period. Their disappearance in great part arises from the encomienda system, which was the first step toward the colonization of the island. [147]

The original inhabitants served as the first recipients of the injustices of the color-coding system on the island. Three different groups of people, the Ciboney, the Taíno-Arawak, and the Caribe inhabited the island when Columbus arrived, and it is estimated that upon his arrival there was a population of approximately 500,000, but by 1550, only 500 remained. The kindness and hospitality that the indigenous inhabitants offered the Spanish was rewarded with extermination. In order to justify the conquest and colonization, the Spanish used religious differences (among other things) as a principal reason for subjugation. The inhabitants were viewed as infidels, heathens, and cannibals who needed to be civilized; accordimg to Cambeira, the idea of civilizing the natives extended the gap between the

---

[147] The encomienda was a feudal system established by the Spanish Crown, which entrusted land and indigenous servants to the colonists. The system enslaved the indigenous population, which was exterminated by 1550. In essence, the encomienda system was a form of human exploitation and subjugation. Although men like Bartolomé de Las Casas (1484–1556) objected to the ill treatment of the Indians and in part was successful because as a result they were not enslaved. However, it opened the door to the enslavement of Africans. According to Pagden, the "the Indians, unlike the Africans, were vassals of the crown of Castile, and the crown took such classifications seriously" (33); this is how the Spaniards justified the enslavement of the Africans.

superior and inferior people. (Cambeira)

With the extermination of the native people and the growth of the sugarcane business, the Spanish Crown agreed to the importation of African slaves. Slaves were black and of African descent and were considered property with a legal sentence to servitude. The issue of miscegenation resulted in a racial hierarchy with whites at the apex, free individuals of color in the middle, and blacks at the bottom. Each group understood the boundaries and restrictions, and usually moved within these realms; obviously there were no restrictions for whites. Mix-bloods or mulattos were considered superior to blacks, and within the black group there were subdivisions, those blacks born in the Caribbean and those born in Africa were at the bottom. These subdivisions among blacks are mocked by Jiménez, "tú / tú no eres negro / tú eres de aquí," to illustrate the nonsensical belief in the superiority of Caribbean blacks over blacks born in Africa.

Dominican racial discrimination derives from the colonial color-coding system, which fostered beliefs and practices that are alive today. For instance, the lines, "tú / tú no eres negro / tú tienes dinero," reflect the sentiments of a mulatto and black society, identifying with white culture and the economical implications attached to race. The separations that existed during the time of slavery continue in a socially accepted fashion, and Jiménez uses his personal experiences as a testimony to this condition. [148]

The occupation of slaves was assigned according to the shade of skin color and features. For example, domestic positions and the jobs that required more skill were traditionally reserved for the slaves of lighter skin. Consequently, this provided greater social esteem for these individuals and a lower social and self-esteem for those working in plantations. The race problems increased with the Haitian Revolution (1791–1804), the neighbor next door. During the fight to liberate Haiti, the French–held territory, Toussaint L'Ouverture felt compelled to extend the battle to the east of the island, Santo Domingo (Hispaniola), in order to abolish slavery.

There were various invasions of Santo Domingo: in 1801 by L'Ouverture, in 1804 the French occupied the island, and in 1805, another invasion by Haiti, and by 1808, Santo Domingo was once again under Spanish domination.

---

[148] Blas Jiménez is a poet who has lived in the United States and considers himself black. But when he wrote "black" on his passport application, 'the lady who was writing the passport gave it back to me and told me to put 'dark Indian.' When he insisted, look at me, I'm black, she replied: 'you look like you're eating, you can't be black.' (Winn 286)

However, in 1822, Haiti again invaded Santo Domingo and remained there for twenty-two years. [149]

In 1916, the United States Marines invaded the Dominican Republic with the intention of reorganizing the government, and the invaders remained for eight years, mistreating and killing blacks in the eastern part of the island, without cause. There was preference for the island's northern area, because the people there were much lighter in skin color. The departure of the United States from the Dominican Republic did not mean that the repressive tactics were abandoned, since they managed to leave intact the tyrannical government of the created military leader Rafael L. Trujillo (1930-1961).

The perpetuation of racial discrimination is attributed to Trujillo, who forcefully imposed Spanish culture on Dominicans, while encouraging abandonment of African culture. Relics of his propaganda are evident in Jiménez's

---

[149] More than an isolated cadre of the country's historical analysts and commentators, as well as of the ordinary citizens today, have concluded that much of the contemporary Haitian phobia has its genesis in Boyer's invasion [...] the population of the eastern end of Hispaniola was made considerably más oscura (darker) as a result of both increased Haitian-Dominican intermarriages and the white flight of greater numbers of Spanish colonists from the invaded territory. (Cambeira 148)

poem, because it reflects Dominican way of thinking today, for example, "tú no eres negro / tú eres un negro blanco," expresses how black people have been conditioned to see themselves as white, that is, a sort of white-washed view of their world. "For Blas, [Jiménez] the situation will not change until Dominicans 'grasp our negritude' and say, 'Yes, this is what I am' we haven't been able to look ourselves in the mirror" (qtd. in Winn 292). Jiménez insists on the Dominicans' need to reexamine, reevaluate, and acknowledge their history with a sense of pride.

IV. A Message of Pride and Resistance

Every segment of Caribe africano en despertar addresses a theme and concept that supports the central message of the poet, the enunciation of a positive statement about blacks in the Dominican Republic, a people who, in spite of their condition, have overcome and endured hardships. All the components of the structure are pertinent to the ideological and aesthetic features of the content and context of the collection of poems. Achugar claims that "internal evidence is sufficient to establish the social and historical situation within which and out of which the book of poems is uttered" (632)[150].   In this collection, historical events are important elements that remind readers of events that should not be forgotten. The poem "Guerrillero," and the dedication of the collection, pay tribute to and acknowledge the history of slavery and those who dared resist the established order. They preach a message of pride, "orgullo de cimarrón," and self-love, "negro bello," and, while suggesting an end to internalized racism, supports the continuance of a legacy of resistance. This idea corroborate Fanon's who maintains that [151]

The revivification of the historical incident (escaping of a slave) gives a reminder of a heroic act of resistance that deserves merit and recognition. Furthermore, the historical event serves to invigorate, strengthen, and highlight the overall message of the collection.

------

[151] … the gangster who holds up the police set on to track him down for days on end, or who dies in single combat after having killed four or five policemen, or who commits suicide in order not to give away his accomplices—these types light the way for the people, form the blueprints for action and become heroes…. If the act for which he is prosecuted by the colonial authorities is an act exclusively directed against a colonialist person or colonialist property, the demarcation line is definite and manifest. The process of identification is automatic. (69)

The dedication adheres to Kubayanda's theory of "maroon literature," which claims (125)[152]. The dedication is as follows:

> A mi abuelo, el viejo
> FELLLO
> Quien siempre fue
> Un negro bello
> (18..–1982)
> (Se fue pero nos dejó
> su orgullo de cimarrón).

The theme of cimarrones or runaway slaves is vital, because they represent the initial significant role of resistant forces in the Dominican Republic. The fiercest rebellions of this time date back to the era of Cacique Enriquillo, who waged fierce wars against the Spanish during the years 1519–1533.[153] As a very astute leader, he organized and gathered communities of Taíno men and women around the Bahoruco Mountains to rebel against the Spanish. Joined by willing and able runaway slaves he launched fierce rebellious

---

[152] "the maroon consciousness appeals to a new discourse vital to a new thinking and to the expression of a revolutionary stream of writing in Latin America"

[153] Enriquillo's rebellion is chronicled by Bartolomé de Las Casas (1484–1556) in his Historia de las Indias (1559). Manuel de Jesús Galván (1834–1910) retells this story in his historical novel Enriquillo of 1882.

acts against the cruel system of slavery. He placed the women, children, and the elderly in safe locations, in order to launch guerrilla attacks against the properties of the Spanish. "Enriquillo was successful in establishing fortified enclaves and strategically located outposts that provided an advance–warning system" (Cambeira 61).

By obstructing transportation and communication, he brought to a standstill the economy of the island. Even though Enriquillo's forces were eventually suppressed, his legacy lives on.

The runaway slaves continued to form fierce mililtias in the mountains. These bands of cimarrones instilled fear in the hearts of Spaniards who realized that the runaway slaves could easily outnumber them. The cimarrones established communities called manieles and organized them to function as well as any other. They offered homes to the runaway slaves and also served as fortifications for revolts against the Spaniards. "The residents of the alternative community—a society within a hostile and noninclusive larger society—were attempting to reconstruct the values and patterns of their forebears, who had come from a number of different African ethnicities" (Cambeira 74). The original freedom fighters, the cimarrones, audacioulsy resisted the system that sought to enslave them, and consequently enshrined a heroic legacy among the oppressed.

The poem "Guerrillero" parallels the idea and sentiments of the dedication of this collection, to a runaway slave, Jiménez's honorable grandfather who represents courageous resistance, tenacity, and adeptness to elude captors. According to Rosario–Candelier, [154]

For this reason the poem embodies the panoramic view of a cimarrón, living in the wilderness and praises the events that contributed to the history and identity of blacks in the Dominican Republic,

> La niebla entre los picos
> una refrescante humedad penetra mi alma
> Yo
> los pinos
> la soledad
> y mi libertad de cimarrón
> [1] Observando
> el indio sufre en deseos
> viviendo en querer ser blanco
> olvidando su cultura
> olvidando su historia

---

[154] los rasgos culturales negros existentes en Santo Domingo no han sido valorizados del todo, ni en todo su alcance. Pese a que están ahí, se niegan, se ocultan o se subestiman sus manifestaciones. (30)

olvidándose

Observando

el indio sufre en deseos

viviendo en querer ser blanco

olvidando su cultura

olvidando su historia

olvidándose

La niebla entre los picos

la muralla que protege mi mundo

Yo

los pinos

la soledad

Y mi belleza de cimarrón

The insubordination necessary to resist the dominant order results in a praiseworthy struggle for freedom and self-preservation. Fleeing, the runaway slave ponders and conscientiously observes his surroundings and those factors that have shaped his life. The poem manifests a concern for the possibility of blacks facing the same fate that befell the extinguished Taíno Indians. The leitmotif "olvidando" alludes to the extinction of culture, history, and a sense of the vanished self as a result of the Taíno's tragic destiny. Jiménez forms a parallel between the demise of the Taíno culture and the disappearing African culture as the slaves assimilate into the mainstream. [155]

---

[155] Observando

The power of resistance and preservation reflect the journey of the individual passing through another stage of his life. The mountaintops and the wall, "la muralla" while they symbolize the depth of his courage, they also separate the two worlds, one of servitude and the other of freedom. The movement toward the world of "rational consciousness" entails a "self-consciousness [that] knows itself to be reality in the form of an individuality that directly expresses itself, an individuality which no longer encounters resistance from an actual world opposed to it..." (Hegel 217). The

---

el indio sufre en deseos
viviendo en querer ser blanco
olvidando su cultura
olvidando su historia
olvidándose
Observando
el indio sufre en deseos
viviendo en querer ser blanco
olvidando su cultura
olvidando su historia
olvidándose
La niebla entre los picos
la muralla que protege mi mundo
Yo
los pinos
la soledad
Y mi belleza de cimarrón

consolation he finds in the mountains and "la muralla que protege mi mundo" imparts a sense of consciousness of having proudly gained his freedom, "belleza de Cimarrón."

V. Reconstructing Identity

Numerous positive images and concepts throughout the collection counteract the negative elements in order to produce a healthy feeling of self–esteem. Deviating from the traditional literary model in which submission played a major role, the poems analyzed in this section responsibly point to, promote, and favor an authentic consciousness documented in the opening quote from the collection of poems by Marley, who acknowledges that blacks all over the world need self–identification.

> El africano ya no se reconoce.
> En Jamaica es jamaiquino,
> en Cuba él es cubano,
> en Alemania, alemán
> en los Estados Unidos, americano
> ya no se reconoce el africano.

The hyperbaton "El africano ya no se reconoce... ya no se reconoce el africano" accentuates the unrecognizable condition of the transplanted "africano." The geographical locations Jamaica, Cuba, Germany, and the United States represent the places to which the Africans have been dispersed and have had to withstand acculturation and the assimilation processes, which gave birth to an unrecognizable African, "africano [que] ya no se reconoce,"[156] who (Jack 67)[157]. Carlos Deive agrees and adds, [158]

The quote highlights the precarious and disappearing black identity that must be delivered from obliteration. The idea that the "africano ya no se reconoce" subtlety suggests, surrenders to, agrees, and accepts with passivity a state of resignation. The allusion to transplantation implies a waning

---

[156] "Acculturation occurs when two or more cultures come into contact [...] in that contact domination and control, conflict, resistance, adaptation, assimilation and other developments may take place, thereby threatening the wholeness of the weaker Other" (Kubayanda, The Poet 34).

[157] "has split himself in two [and] is in exile from himself"

[158] ... desarraigado de su tierra y transplantado a un nuevo habitat, integrado a una sociedad que no era la suya y en la que se hallaba en un estado de absoluta subordinación económica y social, el negro africano vio así destruida su organización tribal y política, sus formas de vida familiar, su sistema de valores, y en fin, sus patrones culturales originales. (qtd. in Alemán 1: 26)

identity resulting from the acculturation process experienced by the oppressed, an idea contrary to Leopoldo Zea's ideal of how the combining of different cultures should be accomplished; he states, [159]

Understanding the objective of the oppressor to divide and conquer, Jiménez delineates and assembles measures to dissolve and overcome partitions and replace these with connective forces for the purpose of arriving at a consciousness of identity. Jiménez exhibits some concepts that appear to be negative and discards them by presenting positive alternatives. The poems analyzed in this section demonstrate a consistent effort toward the removal of negative ideas, images, concepts, and beliefs that perpetuate "supremacist attitudes and values" (Hooks 182). The various poems contest this belief in ineptness.

The poem "Una hermandad que sólo se ha soñado a medias," demonstrates how negative elements that have played a major role in the Caribbean, can also be seen from a positive perspective. Essentially, the poem is the refusal of negative elements as possessing solely nihilistic qualities. The

---

[159] De lo que se trata es de comulgar la cultura del blanco, la cultura europea u occidental, así como toda expresión cultural sin que por ello se deje de ser hombre concreto, negro o el ser latinoamericano. (70–71)

poet highlights adverse, negative, and dissenting factors to illustrate that those elements, as calamitous as they have been, have also been links to optimistic alternatives for the Caribbean islands. For example, the lack of a common language [160] The defeat of dictatorial repressive forces and their tyrannical abuses underscores the people's ability to revolt against and transcend adversity. The reconstruction of these historical events help the people "… recover and relocate past events and what they meant and still mean" (Cox 33).

> Caribe   poco a poco te tragaste a los Batistas
> la furia de tus aguas apagó el sonido de las balas
> que al penetrar la carne de Trujillo liberaban media
> isla.

Specifically, in the case of the Dominican Republic, the end of the Rafael L. Trujillo regime signifies triumph, and a new beginning for the people, because he is remembered for racist attitudes and policies originally forged by the

---

[160] … que no puede comunicarse en el habla" and the ethnic differences among the slaves did not hamper the liberation of the Haitian people in 1804, since "the different African cultures and linguistic groups, [. . .] agreed among themselves to launch the bloodiest war of liberation in America…. (Benítez-Rojo 162)

colonists.[161]

Trujillo opened the doors for white immigrants for the purpose of whitening the race (blanquear la raza), and he is quoted as saying: "a great quantity of immigrants of the white race is needed. The immigrants shall be Spanish, Italian, and also of French origin" (qtd. in Cambeira 185). The words "tragaste, apagó, enterrar," in the poem symbolize an end to negative values enshrined in the hearts and minds of the people by oppressive and repressive forces, and they are contrasted to words such as "liberaban, vida, creador, mañana" which suggest the potential for a transformation. The same region that gave birth to dictators Trujillo, Duvalier, and Batista, also produced great leaders like Eric Williams. [162] [163]

---

[161] Trujillo fue el útero de lo dominicano, tal como hoy lo entendemos. Las fuerzas centrípetas que generó su regimen de violencia y forma dio lugar a la realidad dominicana [. .]. Esa imagen semi-rural, apacible, con merengue y sancocho, pesimista, ingenua y profundamente criolla, creadora del indio para ocultar el mulatto, es hechura del trujillismo. (qtd. in Cambeira 3: 38)

[162] Eric Williams (Prime Minister of Trinidad 1961–1980) believes that the Caribbean, because of its geography is "… one world [.. .]. But in intellectual, as in political matters, the Caribbean is a geographical expression. There is no history of the Caribbean area as a whole. Indeed, histories worthy of the name exist for only a few of the Caribbean territories" (11). He claims that the goal of his book *From*

Dissimilarity should not disbar any island from the Caribbean alliance, an alliance formed on the basis of sharing the Caribbean Sea. The Caribbean Sea serves as what Deleuze and Guattari term a "rhizome," [164] in that "everything is linked to everything" they claim that, "the alibi of a process in which everything one does can be something that one can pretend is politically engaged... the rhizome [is] an endless pattern in which everything is linked to everything [. . .]" (Deleuze,Guattari XXVI). [165]

    ¡Oh, Caribe mar violento!

Columbus to Castro: The History of the Caribbean 1492-1969, "is the cultural integration of the entire area, a synthesis of existing knowledge, as the essential foundation of the great need of our time, closer collaboration among the various countries of the Caribbean, with their common heritage of subordination to and dictation by outside interests" (12).

[163] En tu magia lograste enterrar al viejo Duvalier y

darle vida a un Eric Williams

mar creador de sueños

hoy tu gente se divide

en Cuba pro-ruso, en Granada pro-cubanos

en Santo Domingo pro-gringo, en Puerto Rico-

norteamericanos

[164]A rhizome is an underground mass of roots or a stem very leafy on the surface.

The existing divisions should be avoided for the formation of a brotherhood, which would lead to a conjoined nation, "una nación," because [166]

The utilization of all resources within reach is imperative in order to eradicate whatever continues to hamper solidarity. History has proven that relying on available resources has its benefits. The slaves who fought in the Haitian Revolution "...rebelled not just because they had unbearable living conditions [. . .] but also because the greatest voodoo loas (Legba, Ogoun, Damballah) had willed it so" (Benítez-Rojo 162).

---

[166] ... the more a region or area is broken down into 'local communities'... the alienation is intensified.... These focalized forms [...] hamper the oppressed from perceiving reality critically and keep them isolated from the problems of oppressed men in other areas. (Freire 138)

se sentirán como hermanos
que la sangre son tus aguas

As the rhizome has subterranean roots, and the sea whose waters link "todas las islas hermanas," the Caribbean Sea unifies the islands; in spite of divergences the chief convergence is the Caribbean Sea, "… la sangre son tus aguas."

The poem "Un negro que pelea con su mar" reflects the disapproval of a poet trained to write beautifully and poetically. The tension expressed in the word "pelea" in the title suggests the ongoing struggle for justice, as well as that of a writer trying to overcome restrictions of the literary canon. The struggles against conditions that continue to deny and denounce the development of national identity are of chief importance in this poem. The poet takes offense when having to comply with patterns of the dominant order in order to be considered a legitimate writer. Compelled to write following the standards of the canon, the poet discerns that beautiful words do not diminish the harshness of a bad situation, however poetically expressed: "¿cómo puedo escribir hambre con letras de primera?" The hardships, the pain, and the hunger cannot be beautified.

¡Coño Caribe!
para ser escritor tengo que imitar lo pasado
decirlo en frases bonitas
con palabras adornadas
que tu hombre muere de hambre
[1] Para ser escritor tengo que cantar
odas a mares extraños
decir qué civilizados son los hombres de otros mundos

Feelings of frustration and anger permeate the poem as it addresses with scorn the reverence for the world considered "civilized." The poet acknowledges as well as rebukes the idea that a respected writer must follow the ways and criteria of "extraños" and "otros mundos," because they are considered civilized.

Para ser escritor tengo que cantar
odas a mares extraños
decir qué civilizados son los hombres de otros mundos

Relying elsewhere for approval minimizes native values, contributing to questionable self-esteem among the people. Speaking directly to the Caribbean Sea, he exclaims,

¡Coño Caribe!
siempre de ellos
siempre para ellos
nunca de tí

nunca para tí

mucho menos para mí

mí

mí…

¡Coño Caribe!

Distaste for the disparities that exist between the oppressors and oppressed is cause for protest. The exclamation "Coño Caribe," followed by "siempre para ellos," always for them, which is juxtaposed to "nunca para tí," never for you, underlines the resentment towards disproportionate conditions that consistently counteract development and growth of blacks within society. The line "mucho menos para mí," much less for me, expresses personal displeasure, a sense of urgency, and imparts responsibility on the reader.

The Caribbean man invalidates his own culture as he aspires to embrace the world of the oppressor. The poem "Tú hombre Caribe" illustrates the Caribbean man attempting to enter the world of the "other," through acceptance, and criticizes this attitude, because during the process of entering the world of the "other," he spurns his culture for one in which he will always be considered inferior. Albert Memmi agrees that the oppressed (9)[167].

---

[167] "… knows also that the most favored colonized will never be

Nevertheless, the oppressed attempts to enter this world believing in its cultural, social, and economic benefit. [168]

Absorption by the "other's" world does not entail acceptance because he is still considered one of African descent, a santero and a palero.[169] Vacillation between these two worlds, the oppressed and his own, exemplifies the concept of recombination, the (Esteva–Fabregat 5)[170], a process more common among individuals than groups. These individuals tend to fluctuate between two cultures; they adopt the ways of the mainstream culture but never fully renounce their own culture, and they take advantage of different aspects of both cultures whenever convenient.

---

anything but colonized people, in other words, that certain rights will forever be refused them…"

[168] Se educa intelectual

pero lo pintan santero

saca melodías del piano

pero lo llaman palero

[169] A santero is one who practices the syncretized religion, (West African based religions and Catholicism) Santería. For more details see chapter one. A palero is one who plays a unique drum of Congolese origins.

[170] "conscious use of elements of two or more cultures within a single personal behavior for the purpose of carrying out a more efficient social action"

Driven by the illusion that he will be successful through acceptance into this world, the oppressed tends to denigrate and reproach his very existence. In a delusional state of mind, this individual regards the "other's" ways as better and superior, a regard that drives him to resent anything that is not of that world. For instance, as the oppressed honors the "other," in this case, "el norte," he believes that everything in the other world will be better even though he continues to resort to his cultural traditions whenever beneficial.

> Te acercas al norte
> rodeado por la niebla
> observando las flores de las gramas del verano
> como un universo que muere.

The poetic voice establishes familiarity by referring to the oppressed in the familiar "tú" form for the purpose of persuasion. The oppressed in a muddled state of mind, believes he ascends to a higher echelon of society by approaching the ways of the oppressor. Instead, he distances himself from his own identity, consequently, suppressing his own existence "como un universo que muere."

Falsely believing that salvation from ignorance and upward mobility in society rests on outside influences, the parents take on the task of imparting these ways to their children. Profoundly imbued in oppression the Caribbean man, a prisoner of self–deception, dreams of the world of technology or economic power, while destined to live a life fit for flies and rats, "moscas, ratas." [171]

> Enseñas a tus hijos a sonreir
> pájaros metálicos en los cielos
> cerebros metálicos en las mentes
> y las moscas
> y las ratas
> y el hombre con sus verdades

The oppressed prefers to coexist in alliance with the oppressors, because for him it signifies dominance and power. However, the system forces him to remain within his own sphere, "sus verdades." He will not be allowed to enter this "other" world; he must remain a "prisionero de tu destino." Finally, the poem ends with a pessimistic tone "Enseñas a tus hijos a no sonreir," that contradicts Esteva–Fabregat's notion of the concept recombination as desirable and beneficial. Jiménez illustrates that as the oppressed adopts the world of the oppressor and continues to acknowledge the richness of his own culture, he continues to be considered less than favorably by the dominant order, and he/she will continue to struggle "luchan ellos," as you

---

(the parents) watch in horror "tú tiemblas."

VI. Affirming Identity

Introspection fulfills the most basic needs to those searching for answers in their quest for identity. The poems analyzed in this section support the idea of self-examination, an exigency vital to combat what Bell Hooks calls the "devastating psychological consequences of internalized racism" (175). The epigraph "Debido a una inesperada y saludable revolución interior, ahora rindo honor a mi fealdad repugnante" (37), by Aimé Césaire, opens the second book of the collection of poems. A "saludable revolución interior" requires a dissembling process of the "internalized racism" (Hooks 175) in order to reconstruct a self-image based on acceptance and black pride. It stresses an inner scrutiny similar to a catharsis exercised by the oppressed for the purpose of altering current beliefs, a state of mind, or social and economical conditions that have damaged the self-image of blacks. [172]

---

[172] The aim now is not simply access to representation in order to produce positive images of homogenous communities.... Nor is the primary goal here that of contesting stereotypes - though contestation remains a significant though limited venture [. . .] black cultural workers must constitute and sustain discursive and institutional networks that

The poem "Todo Negro" encourages spiritual evolution that acknowledges and accepts everything pertinent to this culture through confrontation, which entails an analysis, evaluation, and the creation of a new criterion. As an affirmation of black consciousness it suggests an introspective self-analysis for the purpose of reconsidering and promoting a new self-image based on being black. The transformation is from the traditional view of the black self-image to a modern one based on pride.

¿Todo negro?
sí, todo negro
las nubes negras tengo por alas
las noches negras son mi morada.
¿Todo negro?
sí, todo negro
vivo mis ritos que no comprendes
de ritmo traigo mi son candente.
¿Todo negro?
sí, todo negro
uniendo suerte con mis hermanos
creo mares negros, mares humanos.
¿Todo negro?
Sí, todo negro

---

deconstruct earlier modern black strategies for identity-formation [. . .] and construct more multivalent and multidimensional responses that articulate the complexity and diversity of black practices in the modern and postmodern world. (West 20)

un mundo nuevo vamos tejiendo

un mundo negro sin los lamentos.

¿Todo negro?

sí, todo negro…

Nature, the clouds, and the ocean symbolically serve as a backdrop to the poem, its immense power conveys the transformation of distortions and prolific possibilities for change. For instance, the clouds represent a constant "metamorphosis" (Cirlot), which matches the four stages the individual must endure in order to attain consciousness, and the ocean configures the obtainable, because it (Cirlot 241)[173], which coincides with the message of this poem, an affirmation of black pride.

The response "yes, all black" to the question "are you all black," while an affirmation of black pride, becomes a response to the imposed identity of "dark Indians" which Jiménez considers a (Winn 89)[174]. The acceptance of this identity by the individual characterizes the stage of "stoicism." In order to validate inherent cultural traditions distinct from the "other," the poetic voice proclaims "vivo mis ritos que no comprendes." Although these rituals are

---

[173] "is regarded traditionally as the source of the generational of all life [….] the sum of all possibilities"

[174] "… racist attempt to render Dominican blacks invisible"

foreign to some, they have played a major role in history and should not be discarded simply because they are different. For instance, during the Haitian Revolution, which started in 1791, the legendary Mackandal, originally from Guinea, convinced the Haitians of his magical powers, which inaugurated his legendary status. He organized slave revolts against the slave masters and, although he was killed at the stake, his alleged immortality remained a determining factor in the future preparation of the revolution. L'Overture, also known for believing in the power of voodoo, resorted to it during the revolution, although afterwards, he shunned these rituals in order to be accepted as a (Benítez–Rojo 162)[175].

The poetic voice articulates a language that refuses to accept the suffering and the image imposed by the racist supremacist. Transformation and reconstruction may be attained through solidarity, expressed in the poem as follows: "uniendo suerte con mis hermanos / un nuevo mundo vamos tejiendo." Furthermore, the line, "un mundo negro sin lamentos," a black world without lamentations, proposes viewing history from its proper perspective, and not from a

---

[175] "civilized man"

grieving or shameful perspective, because [176]

Through an attained "ethical awareness," the oppressed reaches consciousness by arriving at the stage of "rational consciousness," which allows the individual to placate his dual existence and attempt to forge one in agreement with his/her cultural, racial, and national identity.

Stripped of history, language, culture, and bound by the patterns of the "other," the Dominicans are urged to authenticate their national identity. Resurrection of black culture, ideology, and identity should be the quest of the people. The poem "Cántame poeta negro" implores blacks to abandon the ways of the colonizer and revivify themselves through their own cultural, racial, and national moorings. Structured in seven verses; the first begins with the refrain "cántame poeta negro," a command (the informal tú). The poetic voice speaks directly to the people, "déjame sentirte Negro," encouraging them to feel proud of their ancestry. The switch to the first person singular, in alternating verses, has an inclusive effect. That is, the phrase "estoy sin" confirms that I, too, am a prisoner of the pitfalls and

---

[176] ... shame is a positive emotion insofar as it embodies an ethical awareness of the shameful, whereas "shamelessness" involves a flouting and insulting of ethical standards. (Gross and Walzer 87)

destitution affected by colonialism. [177]

Clamoring "cántame" and "déjame," the poetic voice demands that you (the Dominican oppressed) sing your song to your own tune, with your own lyrics, and with your own voice because; I want to feel and hear you. The time has come for you to stand up, take charge, and free yourself from the shackles that bind you to ways of the "other."

In the following verse, the lines vary between "I do not have," "estoy sin," and "I am hungry," "tengo hambre," in order to disclose the feeling of inadequacy and disenfranchisement among the people. This verse expresses a craving that must be saciated with knowledge of self "tengo hambre de conocerme." [178]

____

[177] Cántame poeta negro
cántame tu canción
déjame sentirte negro
déjame sentir tu voz…
[178] Estoy sin ideologías
tengo hambre
estoy sin educación
tengo hambre
tengo hambre
tengo hambre de conocerme
de observarme

In order to retrieve and restore a debased and plundered culture, disclaiming the teachings of the "other" is essential. The people have substituted their own culture for that of the "other," and while the cry, "estoy sin ideologías… educación… historia…" acknowledges this fact, it also appeals to a new indoctrination that reflects their African ancestral heritage. The poem emphasizes the repudiation of the ideology, education, and history of the "other" as the first step in the movement towards resurrection of an identity. An idea, which agrees with that in Marley's "Redemption Songs," which stresses the trauma, suffered during and as a result of the hardships of the middle passage. He writes [179]

The most oppressive force lies in not knowing oneself itself. Although the oppressor has instilled his ways

---

de nacer de nuevo

[179] Old pirates yes they rob I
sold I to the merchant ships
minutes after they took I from the
bottomless pit
but my hand was made strong
by the hand of the almighty
we forward in this generation triumphantly
all I ever had is songs of freedom…
emancipate yourselves from mental slavery
none but ourselves can free our minds…

in the minds of the people, the responsibility for dispelling cultural brainwashing rests with the oppressed: "… tengo hambre de conocerme / de ver el verdadero opresor / de conocer la libertad interior." Through personal accountability, the people should dismiss the hunger, "hambre," of knowing oneself and replace the "other's" ideology with one that reflects a black identity. The play on words "hambre" and "hombre" accentuates the desperate need of the black man to restore his own identity. [180]

The poem also ends with the refrain, "cántame poeta negro" which recapitulates the idea of self-worth with the hope of persuading the people to resurrect, a new birth of culture, history, and ideology must begin within the people; the victims of oppression must stand up and reassert themselves by discarding the shackles that connect them to the ways of the oppressor. The Spanish colonial authorities very early on devised racial categories for blacks and mulattos based on the purity of blood. The notion of self-denial, the rejection of black culture, and the preference for Spanish culture is rooted in the issue of miscegenation. The poem

---

[180] … para olvidar el hambre

cántame

para ser hombre

cántame

"Otra vez…aquí" protests the desire of Dominicans to be white, while denying and disdaining their own African culture. [181]

This idea was perpetuated by Trujillo, who did everything possible to invalidate African culture, thereby, favoring and insisting on Spanish culture. For example, after the massacre of Haitians in 1937, Trujillo started an immigration campaign to encourage white refugees from European countries in an attempt to whiten the race. In fact, he provided land on the northern coast (Sosúa) to German and Austrian Jews (Cambeira). The idea of whitening the race becomes the death of black culture and identity in the poem.

The comparison between withering roses and a vanishing African culture serves to highlight the disappearance of black culture. The comparison metaphorically illustrates the loss of a culture as a rose that withers and loses its beauty as its color fades. In aspiring to

---

[181] Mixed blood came to be viewed as conclusive evidence of what was described as moral deficiency and intellectual inferiority.... Thus was created the color-coding system in Hispaniola that determined a person's socioeconomic hierarchal position: that particular status was based on the degree of Caucasian blood that an individual supposedly possessed. (Cambeira 90)

be white, the people have been conditioned to see themselves as Indian, either light Indian, "indio claro," or dark Indian, "indio oscuro," in order to identify with the other. [182] [183]

Therefore, the death of one race occurs, and acceptance of another emerges, in order to gradually become white, "muere el negro / como indio, en querer ser blanco." The poem rejects such self-denial and the belief that compels one to succumb to the culture of the "other" in order to be considered a dignified individual: "En este pueblo español / civilízase el Negro / con tonos de varios colores."

For the reader to understand the formulation of cultural conditioning and to recognize that it can be subverted; Jiménez employs a unique method that resembles

---

[182] The line "En este pueblo español" becomes a leitmotif throughout the poem to emphasize the yearning of Dominicans to identify with Spanish and not African culture. It is important to mention that the Dominican Republic celebrates its indepence from Haiti in 1844 and not from Spain in 1865.

[183] En este pueblo español,
rosas marchitas por el tiempo
las negras son.
En este pueblo español
muere el negro
como indio, en querer ser blanco

that of an artist putting together a work of art. For instance, the poem traces the death of black culture. As a sculptor who begins his work of art by adding and mixing materials, the poet writes, "como gotas de lluvia / mézclome con mar y tierra," giving the impression of a creation or the beginning of a work of art in the making. In this case, the inception of a new individual, presumes one that will forget the ways of the old country (Africa) and will not accept the ways imposed on him/her in the "new world" by the "other." This transformation process although considered positive, the following phrases, "lágrimas del viejo negro," "suda el negro…" and "escuchando los lamentos" serve as reminders of the hardships not to be overlooked.

The African man removed from his homeland laments the destruction of his tribal customs, language, religion, and cultural identity when a child is born. The antithesis "nació" and "muerto" best reiterates the message, the alienation of one culture for the appropriation of another, the white culture. "En este pueblo español, / lágrimas del viejo negro / por el pequeño bebé" and "el negrito nació muerto" include the testimony by the old black man who acknowledges the outcome of the conditioning process. Everything alludes to the transformation, for instance, the tears of the old man reflect his sorrow upon realizing that the "viejo negro" ways are a thing of the past, and the utterance, "to be born dead," "el negrito nació muerto," testifies to the transformation.

The notion of self-hate stresses the importance of educating and alerting the people of the perils that await future generations if such thinking persists. In order to produce new individuals proud of their heritage and cultural roots, the poem addresses self-denial as a problem urgently in need of a solution, one that should begin with the annihilation of self-hate "se mata al negro por fuera," and the reconstruction of a new self-image "nace de nuevo por dentro."

VII. A New Dawn

The quote by Jean Paul Sartre, "El negro revolucionario es negación porque desea la desnudez completa; para construir su verdad, debe primero destruir las verdades de los demás," (37) echoes the theme of reconstructing the image, an image that has been constructed by the "other" or "los demás." [184]

---

[184] The idea of misrepresentation here is clearly identical to one meaning of ideology, yet it has little to do with what the misrepresented think or

Congruent with ideas of the third book, "En despertar," to awaken or to emerge, the poems "Contracanto para viejos poetas" and "Poeta a destiempo" illustrate a birth of consciousness manifested through creativity that reflects the positive statement that encompasses the collection. [185]

A new era arises through the restoration of consciousness as thoughts of powerlessness vanish. Evolving from a space and time when captivity posed an obstacle, the rupture with this time erases history and replaces it with one

---

believe about themselves or society. Ruling class ideology, as in the stereotyping of workers or blacks by the mass media, does not have to be believed by the ruled in order to be hegemonic. If as Foucault contends discourse is power, then those who can represent themselves and others through discourse are powerful; those who cannot are powerless. The power to represent oneself becomes of major importance; representation by others is, as Rousseau thought, likely to be misrepresentation and perhaps also, as Marx thought, the path to dictatorship. (Brantlinger 110)

[185] History [. . .] refers to the conflicts within larger oppressed minds and afflicted hearts of a real people pertaining to a concrete reality of acculturation.... Their consciousness of history disclaims notions of unbroken continuum or one-dimensional fixity which the Hegelian dictum "master and servant"-- fine product of European speculative philosophy—seems to connote. A Negritude modality of time is inclined to emergence and change and is, therefore, opposed to permanent symbols of hierarchy. (Kubayanda 37)

that corroborates with a living reality. In the poems "Poeta a destiempo" and "Contracanto para viejos poetas," the poet alludes to and acknowledges that other poets contributed, however, he welcomes the coming of a new ideology of future poets. These poems suggest [186]

Both poems illustrate a desire and hope for the literary creativity of the people to take flight. Although similar, one, "Poeta a destiempo" depicts a discourse more direct and pragmatic, while lacking in a scenic backdrop that implies the urgency of the mission by directly addressing the problem. However, in the other, "Contracanto para viejos poetas," nature provides aesthetics and poetic scenery to the ideology of the poet: "Poeta a destiempo" reads as follows:[187]

---

[186] … an invitation to established figures in Dominican intellectual and literary circles to come to terms with the fact that no longer were they the only agents privileged to legitimize the discourse on Dominican identity, its history and literary tradition…. (De Filippis 154)

[187] Escondido en barrios populares porque odias el
silencio
Sin antologías
ni grupos literarios
o puños levantados por las guerras
Sobre el papel viejo que te dio el pulpero
preparas la destrucción de los mercaderes
Poco a poco

The poem calls on people from the so-called periphery of society, "escondido en barrios...," to express their poetic sentiment. Literary talents are not restricted to the educated, the "antologías," "grupos literarios" and "diccionarios académicos"; instead this area of expression welcomes all. Understanding that the most powerfully talented may come from the masses, the poetic voice invites the common people to utilize their talents as tools of resistance. The masses are called to arms through literary expression as another means of war against oppression.

Similar in ideology to the former, the poem "Contracanto para viejos poetas" portrays the youth, "jóvenes," as the literary future. Moreover, it claims an end to the past "ayer," and anticipates the beginning of a new era "futuro" in literary creativity, which will put to rest the discourse, which denied black or African heritage. Although Jiménez mentions no other poet in particular, he infers that the ideology represented in works of the earlier writers was a product of the time, the Dominican poet of the time: "unió sus pasos al tiempo." The influence of the other's ideology hampered creative originality reflective of Dominican culture and identity. Freire considers this a cultural invasion

---

con las palabras que no son de diccionarios académicos
te haces cómplice del tiempo.

which manipulates and [188] write like them. In the case of Dominicans, the matter becomes more complex, as we consider Ana Beatriz Gonçalves' perspective. She states [189] a nation of blacks. Dominicans fought for their independence from the black nation of Haiti, as opposed to the rest of Latin America who sought their own from Spain. For this reason, among others, Dominicans insist on identifying with the Spanish culture, while denying the culture of African descendants.

The following poem manifests a turn of events by suggesting a new approach to the poetry that rests in the hands of the future poets. [190]

---

[188] makes it impossible for the colonized imbued in the identity of other, to write anything reflective of their true own identity. The values of the latter [. . .] become the pattern for the former. The more invasion is accentuated and those invaded are alienated from the spirit of their own culture and from themselves, the more the latter want to be like the invaders to walk like them, dress like them, talk like them (151)

[189] Negam a presenca do negro e sua participacição na formação dominicana. Essa negação é bastante compreensível, uma vez que, ao contrário das outras naçoes hispanoamericanas, que conquistaram suas independencia lutando contra Espanha, a República Dominicana consegue a sua lutando contra o Haiti, (130)

[190] Llena de cuerpos

la vida

Disipando las nubes

The vanishing clouds, "disipando las nubes," symbolize a metamorphosis (Cirlot) about to occur; the poets on the rise may not necessarily know or have a clear ideology, because they are "estrellas [que vagan] sin firmamento," in an empty space. These stars wander around the firmament without signs of a particular ideology; nevertheless, they have reached a healthy level of consciousness, because [191]

The above poem, as well as "Poeta a destiempo," projects a bright and hopeful future for the poets to come. In both Jiménez acknowledges the need for a new form of expression, because that of the past did not fully represent all the people of the island. Nevertheless, Jiménez does not

---

vagan estrellas sin firmamento

Ayer de viejos

futuro de jóvenes

y un dolor profundo al estar vivo

Fue la soledad maldita

unió sus pasos al tiempo

dejó sonrisas en las almas

y sus huellas en los cuerpos.

[191] Consciousness will determine its relationship to otherness or its object in various ways, according to the precise stage it has reached in the development of the World–Spirit into self-consciousness. How immediately finds and determines itself and its object at any time, or the way in which it is for itself, depends on what it has already become, or what it already is in itself. (Hegel 142)

discard the poetry of the past, a product of its time which produced what it was capable of producing at that time an idea expressed in the lines "fue la soledad maldita / unió sus pasos al tiempo." Jiménez acknowledges that although their expression did not totally reflect the people of the Dominican Republic, they cleared a path for future generations: "dejó sonrisas en las almas/ y sus huellas en los cuerpos."

Chapter 4
Retracing History and Replacing Images

The dignity of persons is their ability to contradict what is, to change and be changed, and to act in the light of that which is not-yet. – West [192]

The poem "Mujer negra," by Morejón, from the collection Where The Island Sleeps Like a Wing, traces the history of black people in Cuba from a women's perspective, while it suggests a reinvention and redefinition of the black image. In a sense, it is an (Hartman 73)[193] in that the historical events that surround the text retrace the different phases black people, but in particular black women, have faced throughout the history of Cuba. [194]

---

[192] Cornel West, *Prophesy Deliverance: An Afro-American Revolutionary Christianity*. (Philadelphia: Westminster Press, 1928) 17.

[193] "inventory of memory"

[194] This past cannot be recovered, yet the history of the captive emerges precisely at this site of loss and rupture. In the workings of memory, there is an endless reiteration and enactment of this condition of loss and displacement. The past is untranslatable in the current frame of meaning because of the radical disassociations of historical process and the discontinuity introduced into the being of the captive as he is castigated

The poem is structured in seven stanzas with lines in between and centers around the violent history, the rupture, dislocation, and dismemberment that embodied enslavement and the breach of the middle passage. It depicts the arrival of slaves to Cuba, the initiation process, the acceptance of enslavement, and the abuse by the slave masters. In the first four stanzas, the poetic voice narrates these experiences of adjustment to the new land, and the lines between the stanzas, "me rebelé, anduve, me sublevé, trabajé mucho más, me fui al monte, and bajé de la Sierra," indicate potential transformations for the enslaved, transformations evident in the last three stanzas of the poem.

Morejón concentrates on the loss suffered by the enslaved, while she simultaneously processes the process of transculturation, the fusion of two or more cultures.[195]

---

into the abstract category of property. The Middle Passage, the great event of breach, engenders this discontinuity. Thus the reiterative invocation of the past articulated in practice returns to this point of rupture. In this instance, memory is not in the service of continuity but incessantly reiterates and enacts the contradictions and antagonisms of enslavement, the ruptures of history, and the disassociated and dispersed networks of affiliations.... This working through of the past is a significant aspect of redress. (Hartman 74)

[195] Morejón defines transculturation in her essay "Race and Nation" as the "constant interaction, transmutation between two or more cultural components whose unconscious end is the creation of a third cultural

Precisely in the middle of the poem we notice a shift from the removal of the past to an acceptance of the new land. The historical perspective corroborates Homi Bhabha's theory that [196]

The inevitable removal from the past ("nunca más imaginé el camino a Guinea. ¿Era Guinea? ¿A Benín? ¿ Era a / Madagascar? ¿O a Cabo verde?") and the sense of uncertainty distance the enslaved from identification with

---

whole—that is, culture – new and independent, although its bases, its roots, rest on preceding elements. The reciprocal influence here is determining. No element is superimposed on the other; on the contrary, each one becomes a third entity. None remains immutable. All change and grow in a "give and take" which engenders a new texture." (229)

[196] Narratives of historical reconstruction may reject such myths of social transformation: communal memory may seek its meanings through a sense of causality shared with psychoanalysis, that negotiates the recurrence of the image of the past while keeping open the question of the future. The importance of such retroaction lies in its ability to reinscribe the past, reactivate it, relocate it, resignify it. More significant, it commits our understanding of the past, and our reinterpretation of the future, to an ethics of 'survival' that allows us to work through the present. And such a working through, or working out, frees us from the determinism of historical inevitability repetition without a difference. It makes it possible for us to confront that difficult borderline, the interstitial experience between what we take to be the image of the past and what is in fact involved in the passing of time and the passage of meaning. (60)

Africa, which signifies a remote past replaced by the new land, "tierra, sangre, huesos, otros, igual que yo." Whether brought here from elsewhere, or whether original inhabitants, the phrases "y los huesos podridos de muchos otros, / traídos a ella, o no, igual que yo," affirmatively solidify the bonding with the new land, and consequently the development of a new culture of Cubans regardless of skin color.

The last three stanzas reflect themes that pertain to resistance, achievement, and the glorification of the Cuban Revolution. They manifest the transformations undergone by the enslaved, for instance, the shift from adapting to a new environment to resistance of slavery, participation in resistance movements, and, finally, the struggle for and the acceptance of the liberation of the land that has become theirs. As the beginning stanzas revolve around the themes of acceptance, adjustment, and acknowledgement of bondage, the final stanzas hope, resistance, and revolt, "me rebelé." Our objective becomes, then, to illustrate the consistent tearing down of the remnants of the dominant subordinate attitudes that constituted the formation of black psyche in Cuban society. The poem "Mujer negra" foregrounds and forms the basis of this chapter. The interpolation of the other poems," "Madrigal para cimarrón," "Negro," and "La noche del Moncada," from the same collection, intertextually complement and reinforce the ideas of the poem "Mujer negra" while they corroborate the concept of "redress" (Hartman 76).

With this in mind, this chapter is divided into four sections. The first section "Concepts" will expound on the earlier mentioned concepts of Hartman, "memory and history," "embodied needs and the politics of hunger," and "redress." The second section, "Vanishing Traditions and Passive Resistance" introduces the analysis of the poem "Mujer negra." We will illustrate how the journey through the middle passage affected the initial sense of loss suffered by the enslaved. The section consists of two parts; in the first, we examine the impression of the slave upon arrival to the new land by concentrating on "remembering" and "forgetting," an attribute of the theory of "memory and history" (Hartman 72)[197].

The sense of lost increased with disappearing cultural traditions that once provided strength. In spite of the fact that (Hartman 72)[198] which alienated the African from anything that could foster a sense of identity, the enslaved

---

[197] "memory and history"

[198] "[t]he violence and dishonor and disaffiliation constitutive of enslavement and the radical breach introduced by the Middle Passage,"

refused to relinquish hope. In the second part we introduce a form of passive resistance, the juba. The juba song becomes a subversive discourse that challenges the system of slavery. "Both consumption of that body's possibility and the constancy of hunger are at the center of juba's witty critique of slavery" (Hartman 70).

In the third section, "Resistance and Heroes," Morejón's theme shifts from a sense of loss obvious in the beginning stanzas, to an exhibition of the triumphs and accomplishments of blacks in the final stanzas. In this section, the historical background of resistance focuses on the cimarrones, runaway fugitive slaves, and their places of refuge called palenques. The great feats of runaway slaves provide a stimulant for future generations of revolutionaries. Morejón's tribute to runaway slaves, in her poem "Madrigal para cimarrón," stresses the importance of the cimarrón legacy that induced future generations to resist the injustice of the dominant order. The poems included in this section substantiate the themes that counter the dismemberment suffered by blacks and are replaced by those reflective of a brighter sense of self. For instance, the polemical perspective of the poem "Negro," voids the "other's" view and definition of blacks and furnishes it with one more reflective of black people's view of themselves.

The first perspective is congruent with that of the nineteenth century novels, Gertrudis Gómez de Avellaneda's Sab (1841) and Cirilo Villaverde's Cecilia Valdés (1882), in which black aesthetics depend on the criteria of the dominant order. These novelists depicted blacks as undesirable and white features as the standard of beauty and superiority. However, in her poem, Morejón refuses to allow the African element to be scathed and diminished. She makes adjustments in language, whose [199]

The second perspective manifests the reversal of the language for the purpose of reeducating a collective customarily resigned to the format established by the dominant order. For example, Gómez de Avellaneda's novel describes the mulata protagonist's (Sab's) features as very light skin with "good" hair to agree with those of white aesthetics consequently cancelling those of black beauty. The poem "Negro" cancels the notion of white aesthetics by regarding these disagreeable features as the sentiments and definition of others "tu pelo / para algunos / era diablura del infierno." (72) On one hand, the poem reveals the origins

---

[199] ...function is clearly one of reversal at the level of speech; however, it also raises and nurtures a combative consciousness through linguistic subversiveness. Here its function is the affirmation of the roots of a minority culture. It has a collective value because its goal is to arouse and nourish a collective sensibility. (Kubayanda 119)

of white aesthetics imposed on blacks by "others", and on the other hand, the language employed by Morejón attempts to expunge these beliefs. According to Hooks [200]

In a similar fashion, the novel Cecilia Valdés posits white aesthetics as the standard for beauty. Although this novel reveals the injustices of the system of slavery, (Jackson 468) [201]. The relevance of these novels lies in that "by speaking, opposing the romanticization of our oppression and exploitation, we break the bonds with this colonizing past " (Hooks 205). The negative connotations placed on black aesthetics by the "other" are uncovered, dispelled, and replaced by an alternative self–image based on black pride.

In the fourth section, "The Road to the Moncada Attack," we briefly trace the political history of Cuba and the corrupt leaders who maintained control of an economic

---

[200] The affirmation of assimilation as well as of racist white aesthetic standards, was the most effective means to undermine efforts to transform internalized racism in the psyches of the black masses. When these racists stereotypes were coupled with a concrete reality where assimilated black folks were the ones receiving greater material reward, the culture was ripe for a resurgence of color–caste hierarchy. (178)

[201] "Villaverde's novel is hampered in part because of the white standard, in part because it deals mainly with the position of the Mulattoes and not with black slaves"

system that kept the poor at the bottom of the social, economic, and cultural strata. We analyze the poem "La noche del Moncada," and its myth-making attribute, by acknowledging women's participation and major role in the transformation and revolutionary activities of Cuba. According to Antoni Kapcia who believes that this historical event furnished the faith in the possibility of a revolution; myth played a significant role in the revolution of Cuba in 1959. [202]

---

[202] Myth can thus be seen as the elevation of a symbol into a narrative, and a symbol therefore as the germ of a myth a stage before organic mythification has set in.... The purpose of politico-historical myth is thus clear: to distil what is a complex, and often necessarily contradictory, system of beliefs in comprehensible form – comprehensible because it is expressed in single future, event or symbol with which the collectivity can identify itself readily, since the subject of the myth is seen to express the core value, or values, that constitute the agreed ideology. These values might, for example, be concepts of self-sacrifice, suffering, superiority, or struggle; but what distinguishes a given myth from ideology's values is that the myth is necessarily expressed in personal (human) form, either in a real, a fictitious or a legendary person (for example, an agreed 'national hero,' a historic liberator, a patron saint, a Robin Hood-type figure) or in an event (real or imagined) that involved specific and defined human beings (for example, Dunkirk, Custer's 'Last Stand', the storming of the Bastille or any such event seen to be critical to the formation of the 'nation')…. if the collectivity that adheres to the myth perceives it to be true in its essentials or its message, then it exists as a reality. (Kapcia 25–26)

In conclusion, we demonstrate that, as the beginning stanzas center on acceptance, adjustment, and acknowledgement of bondage, the final stanzas counter these attitudes with a focus on hope, resistance, and revolt. The analysis of the first four stanzas reflects a sense of adjustment and acceptance evident in the poem. The middle section of the poem (the fourth stanza) indicates a shift in consciousness. The last three stanzas relay characteristics of the enslaved who realizes that he/she can transform the reality of captivity through resistance, and the result of this belief became the Cuban Revolution today in progress.

I. Concepts

Hartman asserts that black slaves in the United States had a formula of resistance that was designed to redefine, regain, and restore a sense of human dignity and pride. She attributes various concepts to the restoration of dignity and pride, although for the purpose of our chapter we will be concerned with only three. As a result of the violence of slavery, the slaves were obliged to originate a manner in which to vocalize their needs by (72)[203]. The captive

---

[203] "... implicitly address[ing] the relation of the history of violence and

manipulates the dominant space by addressing the rupture, dishonor, and disaffiliation imposed by the "other" and, by doing so, the captive recreates an identity for self that cancels that created by the dominant class.

The concept of "memory and history" addresses the relevance of the history of violence and the dislocation that compelled the enslaved to redress. In her study, Hartman does not attempt the retrieval of historical, ancestral, or cultural affiliations, although these elements play a role in the poem "Mujer negra"; instead she wishes [204]

The second theory, "embodied needs and the politics of hunger," politicizes the needs of slaves through an expression that challenges the slave system and the masters by

---

dislocation that produced the captive and the possibilities of redress"

[204] ... to consider the everyday historicity of these practices—that is, the way in which the quotidian articulates the wounds of history and the enormity of the breach instituted by the transatlantic crossing of black captives and the consequent processes of enslavement: violent domination, dishonor, natal alienation, and chattel status. Everyday practices are texts of dislocation and transculturation that register in their "perverse lines of origin" the violence of historical process and, in so doing, offer witness. This witnessing has little or nothing to do with the veracity of recollection or the reliability or fallibility or memory. Of concern here are the ways memory acts in the service of redress rather than an inventory of memory. (Hartman 72–73)

means of an art form, in this case the juba song. The juba song's content scrutinizes the conditions of the enslaved by the dominant order. It criticizes it in a manner that may or may not be detected by the one against whom it is directed. It serves as a camouflaged commentary on the injustices of the dominant order, slyly delivered through entertainment in order to avoid punitive retribution. "Redress" the third [205], relieves and redeems the individual as he/she challenges the oppressive dominant system for the restitution of the pained body. According to Hartman [206]

---

[205] Redressive action encompasses not only a heightened attention to the events that have culminated in the crisis but also the transfiguration of the broken and ravenous body into a site of pleasure, a vessel of communication, and a bridge between the living and the dead.... The limited means of redress available to the enslaved cannot compensate for the remedy and preparation. It is impossible to fully redress this pained condition without the occurrence of an event of epic and revolutionary proportions—the abolition of slavery, the destruction of a racist social order, and the actualization of equality. The incompleteness of redress is therefore related to the magnitude of the breach—the millions lost in the Middle Passage and the 15 million and more captured and enslaved in the Americas—and to the inadequacy of remedy. (Hartman 77)

[206] In order to reconstruct a new self the pained body must first be restituted, a process accomplished by the acknowledgement and confrontation of the consequences of the history of violence, the cause of dismemberment, dislocation, and disaffiliation.

II. Vanishing Traditions and Passive Resistance

"Mujer negra"
Todavía huelo la espuma del mar que me hicieron
atravesar.
La noche, no puedo recordarla.
Ni el mismo océano podría recordarla.
Pero no olvido al primer alcatraz que divisé.
Altas, las nubes, como inocentes testigos presenciales.
Acaso no he olvidado ni mi costa perdida, ni mi lengua
ancestral. [207]
Me dejaron aquí y aquí he vivido.
Y porque trabajé como una bestia,
aquí volví a nacer.
A cuánta epopeya mandinga intenté recurir.
Me rebelé.

Bordé la casaca de Su Merced y un hijo macho le parí.
Mi hijo no tuvo nombre.
Y Su Merced murió a manos de un impecable *lord*
inglés.

Anduve

---

[207]The Mandinga tribe is one of the various ethnic tribes
(naciones) that went to Cuba through the slave trade. Eugenio Matibag
claims that there were six different ethnic groups of slaves from the
Yoruba tribe: Lucumí, Carabalí, Ashante or Arará, Congos, Mandinga,
and Gangas. The Lucumí and the Congos were the predominant tribes
or naciones in Cuba. (62)

Esta es la tierra donde padecí bocabajos y azotes.
Bogué a lo largo de todos sus ríos.
Bajo su sol sembré, recolecté y las cosechas no comí.
Por casa tuve un barracón.
Yo misma traje piedras para edificarlo,
pero canté al natural compás de los pájaros nacionales.

Me sublevé.

En esta misma tierra toqué la sangre húmeda
y los huesos podridos de muchos otros,
traídos a ella, o no, igual que yo.
Ya nunca más imaginé el camino a Guinea.
Era a Guinea? A Benín? Era a
                    Madagascar? O a Cabo Verde?

Trabajé mucho más.
Fundé major mi canto milenario y mi esperanza.
Aquí construí mi mundo.

Me fui al monte.

Mi real independencia fue el palenque
y cabalgué entre las tropas de Maceo.
Sólo un siglo más tarde,
Junto a mis descendientes,
desde una azul montaña,
                    bajé de la Sierra

para acabar con capitales y usureros,
con generales y burgueses.

Ahora soy: solo hoy tenemos y creamos.

> Nada nos es ajeno.
> Nuestra la tierra.
> Nuestros el mar y el cielo.
> Nuestras la magia y la quimera.
> Iguales míos, aquí los veo bailar
> alrededor del árbol que plantamos

para el comunismo.

> Su pródiga Madera ya resuena

The poetic voice narrates her first encounter with the new world through the recurring flashback and synaesthesia: "todavía huelo la espuma del mar que me hicieron atravesar," which vividly creates the image of the ship sailing the seas, slapping against the waves, as it concludes the journey of the Middle Passage, a passage which fractured ancestral ties as it uprooted the enslaved. [208]

The words and phrases such as "océano, alcatraz,

---

[208] Now there is a persistent, established theory that contends that the Middle Passage destroyed the culture of these people that it was such a catastrophic, definitive experience that none of those transported during the period from 1540 to 1840 escaped trauma. But modern research is pointing to a denial of this, showing that African culture not only crossed the Atlantic, it crossed, survived, and creatively adapted itself to its new environment. Caribbean culture was therefore not "pure" African, but an adaptation carried out mainly in terms of African tradition. (Brathwaite 103)

divisé, altas, las nubes, inocentes testigos presenciales, costa," (among others) produce the sound of the fricative consonant /s/, which suggests a silent sobbing and murmuring to heighten the sense of loss. Words and phrases, "costa perdida, lengua ancestral, and epopeya mandinga," "confront [ ] head-on the issues of ... forgetting," and reveals that although the past "costa perdida," may be remembered, it may never be revisited.[209] [210]

The poem refers to certain customs, beliefs, and

---

[209]The majority of the slaves that came to the Americas died in this side of the hemisphere; however, there is documentation that some were able to obtain their freedom and return to their homeland. The idea of emancipated Blacks returning to Africa was originated in the United States in 1820 with the American Colonization Society, a society credited with the formation of Liberia. Quite a few returned to Africa, "nada hay más patético que el caso de estos negros de nación (nativos de Africa) que, libertados a costa de infinitos sacrificios, se deciden a regresar a su tierra natal... Aunque no se ignoraba totalmente que antiguos esclavos cubanos habían regresado voluntariamente a la costa de Guinea, con certeza muy poco se sabía sobre ello" (qtd in de La Riva 143).

[210] All the communities to which Black slaves originally belonged had a series of distinctive institutional relationships. But Blacks segregated from their original communities and enslaved either lost their traditional mores or observed them surreptitiously. Thus the plantation, wherever possible, broke the continuity of African traditions, establishing its foundations upon the destruction of every tie or union, including even that of the family.... (Moreno-Fraginals 13)

rituals that immediately suffered rupture; these fragmented
elements of African culture or rapidly vanishing ancestral ties
reveal the process of deculturation, even after having
(Brathwaite 103)[211]. These fragmented recollections disclose
the gradual progress of the process of dislocation. Nature
and the animal's inability to perform an African cultural
tradition prove the effectiveness of the process of
discontinuation, which does not allow the mission of a
particular custom to be completed. In Yoruba tradition
nature possesses all the qualities to take on human
characteristics for the purpose of restoring order and
providing solutions. [The Yoruba] [212]

These customs gain strength from the power of
nature that protects and guides the inhabitants of the
universe. The first living creature, a bird, the narrator
observes upon arrival to the new land symbolizes freedom,

---

[211] "   crossed, survived, and creatively adapted to the new
environment"

[212] ... believed that living persons could transform themselves into
various animals in order to perform both good and bad acts for the entire
group. Afolabi Ojo maintained that these beliefs and behavior were
reinforced by the empirical fact that nature—that is, wildlife, the
elements, and other inhabitants of an environment—constantly informs
individuals' conscious and unconscious lives.... These beliefs obtained
and functioned in similar ways in Cuba.... (qtd in Howard 22)

"Pero no olvido al primer alcatraz que divisé." The attribution of human qualities to the clouds and the ocean foreground the stanza, "Ni el mismo océano podría recordarla," and "altas, las nubes, como inocentes testigos presensiales." Although the bird symbolizes freedom, both animals and nature remain silent witnesses unable to affect the course of history; they do not intervene on behalf of the slaves. Further, since many Africans brought through the slave trade were very young, between the ages of 15–20, the oral tradition relayed by the elders of the tribes became almost impossible to preserve. [213]

The poetic voice demonstrates a yearning for the strength provided by cultural traditions, "a cuánta epopeya mandinga intenté recurrir," but the tradition does not function or does so at minimal capacity; however, the line "aquí volví a nacer" implies a cultural rebirth. The omission of the word attempt "intenté" would imply the accomplishment of this objective; however, the insertion of the word "intenté" leaves in doubt the completion of that mission, thereby, illustrating another discontinuation of a cultural tradition. The following line, "me rebelé," signifies

---

[213] "In bringing only the young, the least cultural members of a society (cultured with regard to accumulation of knowledge and survival traditions), were imported" (Moreno–Fraginals 10).

resistance and rejection of the elements that represent subordination, rupture, and confinement. With each of the lines in between the stanzas, we notice the individual in transformation actively seeking to transform her condition of enslavement.

After laboring and giving birth in the new land, the slave's acclimatization increases as well as the sense of belonging to that geographical space. These experiences legitimize her presence in the new land, her rights to liberty, and full citizenship. The selected words, "tierra, sembré, cosechas," substantiate her affiliation with and connection to the new land. For instance, in the first stanza home is referred to as "mi lengua ancestral," or "costa perdida," however, in the third stanza it's transformed into a slave shack "un barracón," that she proudly built. The experiences undergone in the new land: "esta es la tierra donde padecí bocabajos y azotes," inspire a transformation. The sense of roots and permanence in the new soil affirms the evolving individual's existence through the building and making of a home, "yo misma traje las piedras para edificarlo" in the new territory.

However, the line "bordé la casaca de Su Merced y un hijo macho le parí," reinforces displacement and illegitimacy as it officially and legally makes the captive property and invalidates her existence by refusing to name her child. The line "mi hijo no tuvo nombre," illustrates the illegitimacy and underlines the rupture of traditional Yoruba beliefs in the slave world by the absence of the ceremonial ritual of naming a child in Africa and (Stuckey 197)[214]. Dominance over the captive and the enforcing illegitimacy by refusing to name the child become modes of rupture in the family structure as well as in the cultural tradition.

Morejón's third stanza manifests a transformation to passive resistance. The stanza in between the lines "anduve" and "me sublevé" indicates a conscientious shift, a repositioning, or relocation of the enslaved. She resists the system of slavery by addressing the theme of hunger, an attribute of the juba songs sung by slaves of the southern United States. This form of resistance details the ill treatment of slaves by their owners and the seditious measures taken by slaves to criticize the institution of slavery. This idea well represents the sentiments of the nineteenth century poem presumably written by a slave and reproduced in the twentieth century by Mirta Aguirre. [215]

---

[214] "as for black people not born in Africa, resentment at not having a surname and at having a Christian name of another's choosing were causes for distress"

[215] This passive resistance, as a means of rejecting oppression and channeling the slave's trauma, included simulating obedience while

The poem written by a slave, who actually lived the horrors of slavery with limited hopes and possibilities of change, expresses a humble supplication. Seemingly, the slave seeks approval from the master as she establishes her acknowledgement of his superiority and meekly accounts for the fulfilling of her task and asks, "¿que jora comé?"

> Mayorá su messé
> que cosa bamo jassé
> Yo tumbo la caña,
> yo yena carreta
> y lleva trapiche
> ¿qué jora comé?

The appearance of a docile, begging individual elucidates the submissive attitude and the passive resistance through the performance of the survival task, in the opinion of Megenny, it seemed [216]

---

complying only with the minimum of what was ordered, imperfectly and unwillingly, and directing his anger against his tools…. This indirect, passive resistance instead of confronting exploitation violently atomized and neutralized the effects of coercion. (Damas 28)

[216] … necesario criar ciertas defensas en una sociedad dominada por los blancos, o en forma de barreras para conservar las tradiciones y los patrones africanos o en forma de adaptaciones a la cultura de los dueños, labor que requería la creación de una nueva personalidad para el esclavo. Esta segunda defensa que resulta siendo una protección personal de

Underneath the feigned docility lies a sarcastic tone that complies with the task of the juba performance: to jeer at the master and undercut the system of slavery. Similarly, Morejón's stanza claims that she did not have access to the crops for consumption, "bajo su sol sembré, recolecté y las cosechas no comí." The seeds planted for the crops, on one hand reflect the unjust and scarce issuance of provisions by owners, while on the other, they symbolize the emergence of future generations "un hijo macho le parí" who will rise up, "Me sublevé," against injustice and to demand his rights to citizenship in colonial Cuba.

Both poem and the stanza centralize the theme of hunger and clearly state that none of the gains of their labor were for their benefit. They illustrate (Hartman 71)[217]. The anonymous poem ends with "¿qué jora comé?" and Morejón's stanza ends with the line "pero canté al natural compas de los pájaros nacionales," which suggests a happy,

---

naturaleza pasiva, exige del esclavo obediencia, humildad y fidelidad son los tres pasos necesarios para lograr el establecimiento de cierta amistad con los dueños, lo que podría producir un ambiente mucho más favorable para el que viene luchando por obtener algo de la autoestima que había perdido como ser encadenado. (Megenny 97)

[217] "...the cruelties of slavery, the exploitation of slave labor, and the appropriation of the slave's product by the slave owners. Amid the seeming nonsense of the juba song was a bid for freedom"

complacent slave; however, the following line "me sublevé," blatantly discloses the refusal of and the struggle against injustice and discounts any impression of contentedness on the part of the slave, revealing the progress from passive to active resistance.

III. Resistance and Heroes

"Madrigal para cimarrón"

La cabeza y las manos colgadas, llameantes,
burlando el rastro del Perseguidor.
Los cuerpos sudorosos se lanzan al manigua húmeda.
Qué belleza tan dura tienen sus corazones.
Sobre sus machetes, como sobre ramales,
anidan palomas y jutías,
y el tiempo de sol,
y el tiempo de luna,
y el tiempo de la voluntad
haciéndolos renacer como a niños
como a dulces niños de una libertad ya conquistada.

The cimarrones, runaway slaves, although their contributions seemed great and worthy of praise, they did no significantly change conditions for blacks after the War of Independence (1895-98) in fact, conditions for Afro-Cubans and the poor rapidly deteriorated. Nevertheless, the cimarrón legacy provides the bridge for a new method of challenging the oppressive and repressive regimes that governed the country. [218]

By paying tribute to the cimarrón Morejón acknowledges a movement of resistance that emerged in order to give a new meaning to freedom. Their determination to challenge overwhelming adversity best represents resistance and the struggle for freedom and independence, "Mi real independencia fue el palenque / y cabalgué entre las tropas de Maceo." [219] As early as the sixteenth century up until the nineteenth century,

---

[218] Marronage can be seen as a bridge between the past, tradition, primitivism, and the future, modernism, technology and socialism, but one which stresses allegiance to an identity larger than oneself, membership in a clan, a tribe, a collective group, a community. Stress on ethnicity and tradition have the power to limit or balance individualism of an alienating kind. Marronage lets me be myself in weaving together the best elements of my ancestral past with the facts of my present situation. It gives me self-confidence by relating to a supportive group. (Wylie 49)

[219] Although the belief is that most cimarrones were newly arrived Africans, all enslaved were prone to escape. "There would have been varying degrees of acculturation among the cimarrones, for house slaves as well as field slaves escaped, imported Africans and Cuban born slave populated the palenques." (Brandon 66)

cimarrones began to establish settlements in the mountains. Flight to the wilderness where they built and settled establishments called palenques, {"fundé mi canto milenario y esperanza / aqui construí mi mundo / me fui al monte,"}in secluded areas provided a sense of community, protection for slaves, and a life free of captivity for blacks from different ethinc backgrounds. Moreover, the palenques supplied the apalencados with a base from which they could assemble, plan, and execute revolts against plantation owners.

Ironically, the stratagem, which the planters sought to utilize as a tactic to divide and conquer had the reverse effect among the runaway slaves in their establishments. To circumvent any gathering of common ethnic cultures resulted in a sense of identity among slaves, [220]

The planters used ethnic diversity among Africans as a way of creating friction and separation in order to thwart

---

[220] Large groups of slaves were never made up of Africans of a single ethnic group: that is, of persons of common tribal or cultural origin. In the thousands of documents about African slaves on Brazilian and Caribbean plantations one can observe a general pattern indicating the care with which slaves from various regions, speaking different languages or dialects, with different feelings of hostility towards each other, were deliberately grouped together. (Moreno-Fraginals 7)

any sense of camaraderie; however, [221]

Morejón respectfully honors the cimarrones because they represent a legacy of resistance that served to stimulate and ignite future generations to seek freedom and equality for all people of Cuba. The admiration and respect for cimarrones exhibited in her poem "Madrigal para cimarrones," approves of and exalts the elusive ability and persistence of the cimarrones to keep trackers at bay.[222] Their genius for evading and mocking the slave trackers, "burlando el rastro del Perseguidor," for centuries allowed them to maintain connection with other slaves in plantations as well as other communities of palenques. Through these means of communication they obtained food, ammunition, and information about different events or movements taking place within plantations.

---

[221] Los colonos que querían mezclar las etnias para prevenir alborotos esclavistas habrán desalentado la separación de las organizaciones religiosas en las Américas según las distintas etnias, pero las evidencias que existen hoy en día demuestran que en la mayoría de los casos estas organizaciones persisten existiendo como entidades étnico-religiosas separadas. Ejemplos son… las casas de abakuá de los ñañigos… las casas de los lucumí de Cuba. (Megenney 122)

[222] This poem is dedicated to Miguel Barnet, author of *Biography of a Runaway Slave* (1994), a testimonial account of the life of Esteban Montejo, a 105-year-old runaway slave.

Should [223]

Their willingness to risk living in the wilderness, "los cuerpos se lanzan a la manigua húmeda," rather than submitting to the dominance of slave masters manifested itself through the polysyndeton "y." To reiterate the slave's perseverance to remain free, the conjunction "y" communicates a union or an association to a continual or a recurrent occurrence related to the legacy of the cimarrón. Thousands of courageous blacks including cimarrones filled the ranks of the Liberation Army for the struggle of Cuban liberation from Spain. The mulatto Antonio Maceo, a highly respected freedom fighter who started out as a foot soldier and advanced to the rank of general, provided a high level of confidence and self-respect among slaves and blacks fighting in the War of Independence. He made his command post in the palenque where the women set up makeshift hospitals, workshops, and other services that

---

[223] …they [ ] be pursued by a party of ranchadores [bountyhunters] or by the Holy Brotherhood… they move to other places, no less hidden, of difficult access, where they also clear cutting no roads, but rather they look for paths that the rivers touch, and they wade along for miles on their march, leaving no traces of their passage of foot… They take the precaution of opening, around their palenques, a number of false paths which they sow with sharp stakes made… and they set traps along the roads that they've prepared for their escape…. (qtd in Benítez-Rojo 252)

provided aid to those fighting the war. Maceo, known as the "Bronze Titan," accompanied by other Afro-Cuban military leaders: his brother José Maceo, Quintín Banderas, and Jesús Rabí (among others) attracted many runaway slaves, who had cause to fight in the War of Independence. Contradictions emerged as the relationship between fugitive slaves and insurgents developed. The insurgent leaders encouraged slaves to join the ranks of the Liberation Army for their manpower and because of their cause to fight for freedom, although they, the leaders, continued practicing racism, albeit on a different scale. Some insurgent leaders dedicated not only to achieving the independence of Cuba, but also to the abolition of slavery and the incorporation of blacks into Cuban society remained watchful of the slave's behavior and habits. They expected the black freedom fighters (Ferrer 37)[224] and maintain their subservience. The sentiment of the insurgents did not interfere with the freedom fighter's eager participation in the War of Independence.

Measured by their dauntless valor, "Qué belleza tan dura tienen sus corazones,"many enlisted their services for the cause of independence. Their military proficiency compares to that of the swiftness of the runaway slave

---

[224] "… to acquire some habits of free men in a free republic…"

eluding trackers, "Sobre sus machetes, como sobre ramales," to emphasize the adeptness and merit of the Liberation fighters. In spite of the courage and valor demonstrated by most, the cimarrones fighting the War of Independence side by side with the Cuban Creoles were still treated as inferior human beings. Nevertheless, their participation offered an opportunity for freedom from captivity, a new beginning, "haciéndolos renacer como niños / como a dulces niños de una libertad ya conquistada," since the war gave blacks a new pride in themselves and their African origin (Helg 63)[225] This sense of pride is manifested in the poem "Negro," which subverts white aesthetics commonly present in Dominican society.

---

[225] Men, women, children, and the elderly played a role in the Liberation Army. Many soldiers brought along their families as part of the "impedimentas" groups of family members that followed the Army from location to location. "Elder African–born men who followed their sons or nephews in the war found a new dimension to duties that they had been fulfilling as slaves. They volunteered to do essential but commonplace tasks such as washing clothes, cleaning arms, or doing night watches. They became most resourceful cooks.... As members of the impedimenta, they participated in a process that transformed them into full citizens of Cuba." (Helg 65)

"Negro"

Tu pelo,
para algunos,
era diablura del infierno;
pero el zunzún allí
puso su nido, sin reparos,
cuando pendías en lo alto del horcón,
frente al palacio
de los capitanes.
Dijeron, sí, que el polvo del camino
te hizo infiel y violáceo,
como esas flores invernales
del trópico, siempre
tan asombrosas y arrogantes.
Ya moribundo,
sospechan que tu sonrisa era salobre
y tu musgo impalpable para el encuentro del amor.

Otros afirman que tus palos de monte
nos trajeron ese daño sombío
que no nos deja relucir ante Europa
y que nos lanza, en la vorágine ritual,
a ese ritmo imposible
de los tambores innombrables.
Nosotros amaremos por siempre
tus huellas y tu ánimo de bronce
porque has traído esa luz viva del pasado
fluyente,
ese dolor de haber entrado limpio a la batalla,

ese afecto sencillo por las campanas y los ríos,

ese rumor de aliento libre en primavera

que corre al mar para volver

y volver a partir.

the poem "Negro," Morejón rekindles a sense of pride as she invalidates the traditional viewpoint of "others" (otros, algunos, dijeron) with a language that undermines the perspective of white aesthetics and provides one more representative of black Cuba. The perspective centered on the people, "nosotros," subverts the view of the "other," allowing "nosotros" to take center stage. It cancels the disparaging description of the black man by the oppressor. [226]

The poet subverts the negative connotation of African–based religions as insignificant, barbaric, and inferior by declaring that "others" see it as such. The reference to the religion Santería, "otros afirman que tus palos de monte [227] nos trajeron ese daño sombrío / que no nos deja relucir

---

[226] The maroon text's commitment to the principle of full emancipation constantly comes to the fore through a language that contradicts the textual and political claims of the old raison d'etat, or those of the nascent criollo superstructure. (Kubayanda 126)

[227] The Congo tribes of Cuba consisted of five different groups: mayomberos, kimbiseros, palo–monte (paleros) kinfruiteros, and briyumberos. According to Megenney, the word palo–monte is of Spanish origen "La voz palero proviene del español palo, una referencia

ante Europa," deletes the negative connotation bestowed upon it. The poetic voice dispels the deprecation of this religion by the dominant culture and discourse that represented the eurocentric order, because the black man brought with him his own history, "has traído esa luz viva del pasado." The poetic voice reflects the sentiments of the oppressor when she describes him as disloyal, "infiel," only to counter this by comparing him to the winter flowers that stand upright and firm in spite of the season, "como esas flores invernales / del trópico, siempre / tan asombrosas y arrogantes."

The last stanza clearly denounces the imposition of demeaning and inferior standards that lead to the negative self-image. The reference to "ánimo de bronce" brings to mind Maceo and the likeness of other black men who participated in the various wars and battles, "ese dolor de haber entrado limpio a la batalla," throughout the history of Cuba to pave the way for future generations. The historical accomplishments, "tus huellas," of blacks will be forever praised, "nosotros amaremos por siempre." The poetic voice recognizes that the "other" initiated this attitude and its perpetuation; however, the responsibility of deconstructing this attitude belongs to "nosotros."

---

directa al monte y a los palos sagrados del mismo." (156)

IV. The Road to the Moncada Attack

"La noche del Moncada"

Pasaron treinta años.
Como pasan los cometas en el espacio.
Pasaron treinta noches exactas
y aquella noche fue más noche
porque, tal vez, sería la última
 o la primera noche de una época estrenada.
Los ojos de Abel pudieron contemplarla todavía.
Hasta hoy llega el perfume
de la noche silvestre, duradera,
entre las hierbas de la granjita Siboney
y el brillo de los fusiles navegando en el pozo del patio.

Hasta hoy se escuchan los disparos
que median entre aquella noche grande
donde unos jóvenes comieron, cocinaron, cantaron
y nos hicieron una noche más dulce.
Pasaron treinta años, treinta noches del trópico
y pensar que esta noche yo vivo el privilegio
de contemplar otra noche tan linda,
sin más ni menos luna, sin más ni menos ansias,
otra noche tan grande,
que vive en el aliento de la libertad
mientras respiro ésta, aquella noche,
que merecía verse toda la vida.

Cuba gained independence from Spain only to cede control of its economic resources to the United States. Those who governed the island after the War of Independence were obliged politically and economically to the United States. Havana was considered the playground for wealthy gamblers while the rights of the average Cubans were disregarded.[228] During the puppet dictatorship of Gerardo Machado, known as "The Butcher" (1925–33), [229]

When Machado's dictatorship was overthrown in 1933, the United States backed the military leader Fulgencio Batista (1934–59) in order to retain control over the economy. Batista seized government leadership in an uprising called the "Revolt of the Sergeants" and caused even more difficult times for the proletariat sector of Cuban

---

[228] The United States immediately seized and annexed Cuba through the Platt Amendment of 1902, which allowed Cuba semi-independence while it provided the United States with an opportunity to maintain a military force there.

[229] … this beautiful island nation had become the tropical playground of foreign tourists, U. S. businessmen and financiers, mafia bases, and military personnel stationed at U. S. naval bases. The ceaseless lights of the casinos and nightclubs, the rhythmic sounds of rumba, mambo, and cha–cha–cha, the pristine beaches offering unlimited sand and sun, and the promise of fulfilled sexual fantasies through easy access to voluptuous Cuban prostitutes had lured hordes of North American tourists to the island since the 1920's. (Maloff 24)

society. Recognized by the United States, Batista governed the country through puppet presidents from 1934 to 1952, when he staged another coup d'etat. Prior to this date, Fidel Castro contemplated participating in and working within constitutional politics. He wanted to fight the government of Batista through the political system; however, he later commented. [230]

The strategy to rid Cuba of outside influence and the dictator Fulgencio Batista, who represented poverty, hunger, high rates of mortality, and illiteracy for the majority of the population, began with the plan to attack the Moncada and the Bayamo barracks on the eastern side of the island. The poem, "La Noche del Moncada," expresses gratitude and appreciation for this momentous occasion, because it forever altered the history of Cuba. Morejón pays tribute to Haydeé Santamaría, a woman and active participant in the Moncada assault.[231] The epigraph, *"La noche era más Linda, era como*

---

[230] I began to organize the first action cells, hoping to work alongside those leaders… who might be ready to fulfill the elemental duty of fighting against Batista…. But when none of these leaders showed that they had the ability, the resolution, the seriousness of purpose or the means to overthrow Batista it was then that I finally worked out a strategy of my own. (qtd in Simons 272)

[231] Other women were known to have participated in battles in the hills, some of whom were killed. Santamaría, Melba Hernández, and Celia

algo que merecía verse toda la vida, y a lo mejor que no veríamos más, " a quotation of Santamaría, recalls the eve of the Moncada assault.

Morejón adds to Santamaría's idea of interminability by insisting that it was only the beginning of a new era, "porque, tal vez sería la última, / o la primera noche de una época estrenada." The words, "última" and "primera" symbolize the end of an era and the beginning of a new one rooted in Cuban history, in spite of the Moncada attack's military failure. History tells us that on the day of the attack, the guerrillas gathered a few weapons and dressed in Batista's military force's uniforms for the purpose of arousing confusion and disarray among the Batistianos. The date July 26, 1953 was chosen because officers participating in the Carnival festivities on the 25th of July might not be able to defend efficiently.

Although Castro's forces of nearly two hundred men and a few women were outnumbered, he depended on the (Judson 2)[232] and the hope of gaining support from disillusioned soldiers. The attack, which took place just

---

Sánchez survived and later held high positions in postrevolutionary Cuba. (Maloof)

[232] "element of surprise"

before dawn, was a disaster. Batista's well-trained and prepared forces quelled the uprising, which lasted only an hour. Many of the guerrillas captured were tortured and murdered; Castro himself was captured and much later stood trial.

Considered a failure, this event served as a social myth that propelled future revolutionary activity, because, "hasta hoy llega el perfume." The everlasting effect of the Moncada attack is reiterated throughout the poem by words and phrases such as "treinta años, treinta noches, duradera, hasta hoy, vive, and toda la vida" corroborates the perennial effect of this pivotal occasion, which gave the proletariat of Cuba a reason to believe in spectacular occurrences. Comparing the Moncada episode to a natural phenomenon like the appearance of a comet, "como pasan los cometas en el espacio," stresses the privilege of experiencing an event that may occur once in a lifetime.

Lack of reference to the violence that took place emphasizes the greatness, effectiveness, and pleasure of this night,"… una noche más dulce," that lives forever. Although she mention's "fusiles, disparos, los ojos de Abel,"[233] the poet avoids the violent details of the event in

---

[233] The reference here is to Santamaría's brother Abel who, as a rebel

order to underline the courage of those who gave their lives for future generations, "unos jóvenes comieron, cocinaron, cantaron / y nos hicieron una noche más dulce." Today many, including Morejón, have the privilege of existing with hope of a future, "... yo vivo el privilegio / de contemplar otra noche tan linda." Other significant days "otra noche tan grande / que vive en el aliento de la libertad," surfaced as a result of the Moncada night attack. By not distinguishing between that night and this night, "mientras respiro ésta, aquella noche," the poet asserts that that particular night made today possible, "... el aliento de la libertad."

The proletariat acknowledged its existence in the midst of a societal crisis' a crisis based on the contradictions of that society, and it continued the dream and direction of the Moncada night participants. That is, it saw the possibility of a revolution. This revolutionary consciousness motivated the people to lead a revolution. [234]

---

during the Moncada assault, took control of a hospital. When he realized that the rebels were unable to take control of the Moncada barracks, he continued the fight from the hospital until overpowered by the military. He along with others including his sister Haydée were jailed. When he refused to supply authorities with information, his eye was yanked out and taken to his sister.

[234] The term "revolution" here is taken to mean the radical readjustment

The (Judson 2)[235] characterizes the tone and spirit of the women who participated in this monumental historical event. Cuba's revolutionary guerrilla rebels included a group of women called the Mariana Grajales Platoon, named after the mother of Antonio Maceo, an active contributor in the struggle for independence.[236] Castro has said [237]

---

of class relations, the overthrow of the rule of one class by another, social revolution in the classical Marxist sense. This level of revolutionary consciousness can be achieved by political practice, observation and reasoning. However, such consciousness also includes an element of faith. It includes the conviction not only that such a resolution of contradictions is possible, but also desirable, necessary and imminent. Revolutionary consciousness implies faith and belief in victory, emotional identification with the cause of social revolution, and a belief that social regeneration will be made possible by insurrection and revolution. (Judson 2)

[235] "faith and belief in victory [and] emotional identification"

[236] Mariana Grajales Maceo (1808-1893) along with her husband and nine children lived among the Liberation fighters in the mambí camps or palenques. She ran a hospital and on separate occasions had to tend to her own wounded children fighting the Spanish colonial forces. She died in self-imposed exile in Jamaica. José Martí describes her as he refers to her son Antonio, "he is his mother's son, more than his father's, and it is a great misfortune to owe one's soul; but Maceo was fortunate, because he was born of a lion and lioness. He is losing his mother, the glorious old lady is dying in indifferent foreign parts, and yet still has a girl's hands to caress one who speaks of her country.... She saw her son, covered in blood, and with only ten men, disband 200. (qtd in Franco 49)

The naming of a platoon after a hero's mother concurs with Joseph Campbell's idea that if a historical figure is considered a hero, (Campbell 321)[238]. Further, the application of a namesake such as that of a hero, whether it be Mariana Grajales or Antonio Maceo, motivates a people towards revolutionary action and instinctively gives credence to the myth-making concept, because [239]

The testimony of a Mariana Grajales Platoon member, María Antonia Carrillo who later became the Afro-Cuban Dance Troupe Director and an artist, attests to and complements this idea. [240]

---

[237] I remember that when I organized the Mariana Grajales Platoon—in fact, I took part in the combat training of these comrades—some of the rebel fighters were furious, because they didn't like the idea of a platoon made up of women. (qtd in Maloff 27)

[238] "the builders of his legend will invent for him appropriate adventures in depth. These will be pictured as journeys into miraculous realms, and are to be interpreted as symbolic…"

[239] these early experiences of what would be the core of the Rebel Army took on the characteristics of social myth in that they were compared to the exploits of past Cuban heroes and martyrs. The experiences were seen by the surviving Rebel Army as part of the continuing Cuban duty of national redemption and as symbolic of the character and destiny of the Cuban population as a whole. (Judson 18–19)

[240] I was one of the women who fought in the all-women platoon called Mariana Grajales. It was a beautiful experience. We were all so united

Considered a military failure, Morejón suggests that the Moncada barracks was the root of the struggle of the revolutionary movement. The poem documents the immortality of the night filled with augury of future rebellious events that would lead to the Cuban revolution.[241]

Finally toppled on January 2, 1959, Batista fled to the Dominican Republic, and Castro assumed power. Castro and the guerrilla fighters came down from the Sierra Maestra

---

and so in love with the Revolution. There weren't any bad feelings of rivalry or jealousy among us. I had to learn how to use a weapon; I didn't think I would be able to but I did. The sense of revolutionary fervor that developed us was so strong that fighting back seemed like the only thing to do. It was the only way to get rid of the tyrannical dictator who was torturing and murdering so many of our compañeros. The only thing we cared about was to keep moving forward and keep fighting. We fought in a number of battles near the end of the revolution during the last months of 1958. I will always carry with me, in my heart, the memories of this experience, and the celebration and joy of our victory! (qtd Maloof 65)

[241] ... Cuban Rev. Faustino Pérez commented that the combatants of Moncada "did not achieve their military objectives, but they did achieve their revolutionary objectives..." and in the same vein the Cuban writer Guillermo Cabrera Infante wrote: "The Moncada attack... was a failure from the military point of view. But it was a resounding political success." After July 26, 1953, everything in Cuba became a vast historical moment--brutal, bloody, and inevitable. It was at Moncada that the July 26 movement was born. (qtd in Simons 274)

Mountains, after strategically planning an attack on Batista's regime, "Sólo un siglo más tarde, / … bajé de la Sierra,"[242] to expel outside influence, which prevented equality and development in the country. The ideal of the revolution was to do away with the corruption, "para acabar con capitales y usureros / y generales y burgueses," that plagued the country since the end of the War of Independence (1895–98). Castro's sentiments and words, (qtd in Simons 286)[243] parallel those of the poem, "ahora soy: sólo hoy tenemos y creamos / nada nos es ajeno," which make an autonomous statement based on a sense of pride, and challenge the thought of an invasion by the United States. The image of shackled slaves vanishes as the creation of a new worldview takes shape.

Hopeful and visionary thoughts pervade as one reads "nuestro el mar y el cielo / la magia y la quimera," which envisions dreams without limits in the future. The personal "I," employed throughout the poem, in the last stanza, becomes a collective "we," "nuestra… / nuestros… / nuestras …" to suggest the power of the people. As if the

---

[242] From this section on all poetry quoted will be from the poem "Mujer negra."

[243] "this time it will not be like 1898, when the North Americans came and made themselves masters of our country,"

revolution bestowed on the people the gifts of the "mar," the "cielo," the "magia," and the "quimera," the people see a new horizon in the making. This idea echoes a segment of Castro's speech (qtd in Simons 286)[244]. The oppressive occurrences are replaced with visions of hope, magical events, and festive celebrations that give rise to a new day for the multiracial Cuban existence, a view affirmed by the witness María Antonia Carrillo: [245]

In conclusion, all three writers Ana Lydia Vega, Blas Jiménez, and Nancy Morejón concentrate on a new racial

---

[244] "… but now I am sure that the revolution will be made, that for the first time the republic will really be entirely free, and that the people will have what they deserve…"

[245] For me, personally, as a black woman in Cuba, the Revolution brought opportunities that I'd never even dreamed were possible. In pre-Revolutionary Cuba the only option for a black woman was to work as a domestic servant in the home of some wealthy white woman who lived in Miramar or some other fancy neighborhood, or maybe get a job as a waitress at a third–or fourth–or fifth–class joint. Most of the first-class restaurants and nightclubs preferred to hire white women because of racial discrimination in this country, very few blacks were able to get a university education before the Revolution. Even in my small town the whites strolled in the center of the park and expected us to stay on the edges—that is actually outside the park. I think racism was one of the main reasons why so many of us black Cubans joined the revolutionary forces. The rebels were fighting for a new society based on racial equality and on the equality of women. (Maloof 65)

reality that depicts a more believable portrayal of Blacks. Vega, in order to address her reader effectively, works at narrowing the gap between the text and reader. She addresses national issues fundamentally rooted in colonialism for the sake of clarifying misconceptions. Through the oral quality of her writing, Vega engages her audience, gains its trust and invites participation in her stories. Throughout the story "El día de los hechos" Ong's features of orality are vividly illustrated. For example, to display the negative self-image, Vega utilizes a historical setting that allows silenced voices to be heard. Ong's feature, "close reference to the human lifeworld," allows personal anecdotes to play a major role in storytelling; the reliability of the account becomes greater. For example, the narrator tells her readers (23)[246], and at the end she reiterates (27)[247] Such closeness to accounts establishes eyewitness testimony; consequently, the reader becomes more susceptible to persuasion.

Vega also engages the reader by appealing to communal familiarities. The emphasis on biblical quotations adheres to Ong's feature, "conservative and traditionalist," which permits the narrator more flexibility to combine familiar expressions in order to appeal to the reader. For

---

[246] "sí señores, yo estuve allí..."
[247] "yo lo sé casimente todo."

instance, Vega introduces old familiar themes with a twist to capture the attention of the reader. In the story "El día de los hechos" the allusion to the Cacos rebellion spotlights the central theme of brother killing brother, with the intention of highlighting the historical event. Moreover, the major attention placed on reevaluating how and from whose perspective history is told serves as "cathartic and healing" and contributes to (Cohn 190)[248].

Some writers work from perspectives that mirror their cultural purview, because national, historical, and cultural elements bind reader to text. However, in order to affirm these perspectives, Deleuze and Guattari claim that a "deterritorialization" of the language ensures the thrusting of the language to the limit. The creation of such "deteritorialization" in the language creates a minority language within a major language. Although Zielina agrees, she insists that efficaciousness depends on the "lector informado" of "africanía." The "lector" should be acquainted with the Caribbean, capable of deciphering identifiable cultural familiarities.

The tinges of Santería throughout the story "Encancaranublado" manifest elements of "africanía." In

---

[248] "a future less marked by the hardships that have plagued them"

the midst of a hurricane season the men Antenor, Diógenes, and Carmelo dangerously float around in the Caribbean Sea, and in spite of the erratic and unstable future which they face, hope looms in their hearts. The faith in Santería leaves little room for hopelessness, as manifested in the story through various references and suggestions of Santería, for example, the mention and supplication of Las Siete Potencias Africanas, La Virgen de la Caridad del Cobre, and La Virgen de Altagracia. However, certain associations such as the evocation of the Orishas may not be easily deciphered. According to Zielina, the (32)[249] The allusion to Santería and voodoo confirms the depth of ancestral beliefs, rituals and practices that survived amid the (Esteva–Fabregat 6)[250].

The flavor of "cultural mixing" demonstrates what Vega relays to the reader of her text; it reflects reality and experiences of the common people with a language suffused with (Vega 314)[251], which resembles the "parodia sacra" defined by Bahktin as a (76)[252]. The language reflects the joyous and festive spirit that comprises the soul of the

---

[249]"lector de la 'africanía' tiene que llenar 'huecos,' tiene que suplir, con su experiencia de cultura sincrética...."

[250] "cultural mixing"

[251] "los juegos de palabras..."

[252] "never–ending folkloric dialogic: the dispute between a dismal sacred word and a cheerful folk word..."

people, notwithstanding their condition, as can be seen in the mockery of the illiteracy of Haiti, the rampant racial epithets, and the musical backdrop that serves as counterpoint to the descriptive killing scenes. The orchestration of music in everyday life and the text suggests the idiosyncrasies of Caribbean popular culture.

On the other hand, Jiménez proposes a literature that relinquishes the literary values established by the dominant order by suggesting the deconstruction of the colonial psyche of the Caribbean, specifically that of the Dominicans who, as a result of prejudice and racial discrimination, (Dubois 77)[253]. The power of colonialism caused a decline in morality and dignity among the people, and as a result, they [254]

Although West refers to the issues of African Americans in the United States, similarities exist among the

---

[253] "... could not but bring the inevitable self-questioning, self-disparagement, and lowering of ideals which ever accompany repression and breed in an atmosphere of contempt and hate"

[254] ... face the social breakdown of nurturing systems for children (not just their bodies but their souls), and hence deracinated individuals, rootless individuals, denuded individuals, culturally naked individuals who have lost their existential moorings, who become easily caught within a subculture of violence. (West 119)

oppressed people of the Dominican Republic. The similar tactics of the oppressors almost always breed a "deracinated, rootless denuded" individual destined to a hollow, shallow and disgraceful life.

With this in mind, we have applied the theories of Kubayanda, (stoicism, skepticism, unhappy consciousness and rational consciousness) based on Hegel's theories of (111–119)[255]. Kubayanda's theory is pertinent, because it reveals the passage through which the colonized individual must travel if he/she is to reach consciousness, the most important stage for decolonization. We have discussed the origins and the effects of "negrism" in black Caribbean literature, a fundamental necessity for any research that treats the issue of black identity in the Caribbean. The history of discrimination in the Dominican Republic discussed above serves to clarify the issues of self–hate and to establish the roots of the color–coding system in the Caribbean, which has origins in the encomienda system. Of course, Trujillo did his part to perpetuate the problems of lack of self–esteem by encouraging and promoting Spanish Peninsular culture.

Historical events play a significant role in this chapter, because they remind the reader of the options and

---

[255] "Lordship and Bondage"

alternatives that were available to the people. For example, the theme of the runaway slave offers a sense of pride because of its role of resistance. The reverence and praise of cimarrones provide another perspective to the history of slavery. By dedicating the collection of poems to his grandfather, Jiménez's personalization of the theme provides a sense of authenticity to the reader. It is his way of saying, I knew a runaway slave; yes, we do come from a people of resistant warriors, and the legacy should and will live on.

In spite of the hardships the black people have endured, Jiménez wants to assure them of triumphs that may be achieved. However, he suggests a reconstruction of identity based on self–acceptance and black pride. He discards the division and hardships that exist among the people of the Caribbean by introducing positive elements that will build a new self-image, free of self-hate. (Adorno 89)[256]. Jiménez confronts issues for the purpose of recovering from a nihilistic view of life. Therefore, we view his approach as progressive, since he suggests a reinvention and redefinition of the image based on a fresh criterion.

Morejón also dismisses the traditional beliefs that

---

[256] "The concept of progress is philosophical in that it articulates social movement while simultaneously contradicting it. Social in origin, the concept of progress requires critical confrontation with real society"

comprise negative values, which she replaces with those of a positive spirit. We have demonstrated through the analysis of the poems "Mujer negra," "Madrigal para cimarrones," "Negro," and "La noche del Moncada," her staunch and resolute effort to dismiss the disparaging self–image of black people in Cuba. To do so, we have examined how the violent institution of slavery, which displaced blacks through captivity, obliged them to seek a means of redress. The tearing and peeling off of the dominant subordinate attitudes that constructed the formation of black psyche in Cuban society form the core of this chapter.

The poem "Mujer negra" underlies the entire chapter; however, the other poems significantly support and verify the sentiments illustrated in this poem. The lines "me rebelé, anduvé, and me sublevé," while they convey motion and transition, anticipate an optimism and a commitment to combat subjugation. They send a message of perseverance and hope, evident in the final three stanzas and reinforced by the other poems.

Hartman's theory of "memory and history," "embodied needs and the politics of hunger," and "redress" delineate certain aspects attributable to the restoration of dignity and pride among the enslaved blacks. Although the beginning stanzas revolve around the idea of acceptance and adjustment to captivity, the final stanzas focus on hope, resistance, and revolt for the purpose of restoring dignity. The slaves (and later, poor Cubans) sought and created methods and tactics that addressed the rupture, dishonor, and disaffiliation imposed on them by the dominant order. We have noted the examples of the juba song, which addressed the theme of hunger by lashing out at the miserly master who rationed the distribution of provisions, and the runaway slave or cimarrón, who escaped to the mountains and established communities from which he/she could retaliate against the system of slavery.

The poem "Madrigal para cimarrones," substantiates and demonstrates the determination of the enslaved to resist slavery and fight for freedom and independence. The exalted legacy of the cimarrón is highly respected, because it symbolizes defiance as well as hope for those who refused to submit to despair. Many cimarrones displayed their courage by enlisting in the military forces to fight against the Spanish colonial forces during the War of Independence. Although this service did not grant them the same status as that of the Creole Cubans, it did provide a sense of pride for those fighting for a cause side by side with the military Mulatto leader Maceo. The poem "Negro" confirms the new sense of pride, because it depicts the black man as a solid figure worthy of mention, "tus huellas y tu ánimo de bronce."

The language evident in this poem repudiates the traditional perspective of white aesthetics and replaces it with one based on black pride rooted in self-respect.

The poem "La noche del Moncada" recreates the exhilaration experienced by the participants in this occurrence, even though the assault was considered a military failure. After Cuba gained independence from Spain, changes in conditions were minimal for blacks and poor Cubans. The dictatorships of Machado and Batista, backed by the United States, did not allow economic advancement for the proletariat. To deliver the island from poverty, the Batista regime, and outside influences, Castro and a few hundred Cubans attempted the attack of military barracks on the eastern side of the island, an event which served as a proponent of similar resistant activities, and it inspired the common people to rise up against the injustices of the dominant order that subjugated them.

The faith and belief in heroic acts motivate the people to insurrectionist ventures, as in the case of the Cuban revolution of 1959, today in progress. Moreover, a nation which is born of the people's concerted action and which embodies the real aspirations of the people while changing the state cannot exist save in the expression of exceptionally rich forms of culture. (Fanon 246)

We have noted this richness in the testimony of Carrillo, a woman who participated in the revolutionary struggle and who later experienced and enjoyed the fruition of the revolution through education, an opportunity finally afforded to blacks, and who eventually became the director of the Afro–Cuban Dance Troupe. We believe that a great deal of revolutionary consciousness has its roots in myth. [257]

It bears repetition that the nucleus of the poem "Mujer negra" delineates the history of black people in Cuba, and the first few stanzas concentrate on the loss suffered as a result of displacement, dislocation, dismemberment, and rupture; however, the last few stanzas propose an alternative perspective that counteracts this sense of loss. Moreover, the analysis of the other poems focuses on the removal of old ideas that have shaped the black psyche, ideas that lead to

---

[257] The term "myth" as used here is, therefore, the cohesive set of values seen to be expressed in an accepted symbol or figure, which is perceived by a given collectivity (a class, a society, or indeed, a "nation" -- real or imagined) to articulate the "essence" of all, or a significant component part, of its accepted ideology, and to articulate it in simple, symbolic or human -- and therefore comprehensible -- form. It follows, therefore, that a politico–historical myth is the means through which the "message" of an ideological code is conveyed across time and across a society, to be comprehensible at the individual level, not least because a myth is fundamentally the code expressed as metaphor, converting a symbol normally associated with, and seen as expressing, a code into a more coherent, organic 'message,' with a 'storyline.' (Kapcia 25)

self-hate, and replaces them with those that encourage a positive self-image. For example, the stanzas in the poem "Mujer negra" divulge the details of the process of the dominant conditioning of the enslaved, and the lines in between mitigate these through an inclination that favors self-expression for the purpose of attaining some form of freedom. While the lines in between the stanzas, "me rebelé, anduve, me sublevé, trabajé mucho más, me fui al monte, and bajé de la Sierra," suggest a movement toward liberty, they simultaneously neutralize the stanzas that reflect the process of adaptation to the new land.

Taken as a whole, these verses denote a transformation, a leap to another consciousness, an imperative action that empowers the enslaved and grants him/her the ability to dismantle the shackles, above all, the mental ones. The final stanza glorifies the struggle of the ongoing Cuban Revolution, which embodies (Fanon 246)[258]. Ultimately, the poem ends by reaching a climatic stage, which serves to discount the repressive and oppressive factors of colonialist and pre-revolutionary Cuba, and celebrates and glorifies the Cuban Revolution, which gained

---

[258] "a struggle which mobilizes all classes of the people and which expresses their aims and their impatience, which is not afraid to count almost exclusively on the people's support, will of necessity triumph"

control of all aspects of its national interests. In essence, Ana Lydia Vega, Blas Jiménez, and Nancy Morejón not only address the issue of self-hate through introspection, but they provide alternative measures, which have been successful throughout history to encourage the decolonization of blacks. These writers have indeed tenaciously sought to replace the negative image of blacks in traditional Spanish-Caribbean literature by representing a more authentic picture of blacks, commensurate with their rich culture, traditions, and history.

Bibliography

Adorno, Theodor W. "Progress." Included in Benjamin: Philosophy, Aesthetics, History. Ed. Gary Smith. Chicago: University of Chicago Press, 1989.

Aita, Olga Mariella. "Simone Schwarz–Bart: el mito revelado (Americanidad, etnia y real maravilloso)." Included in La huella étnica en la narrativa caribeña. Eds. Aura Marina Boadas and Mireya Fernández Merino. Caracas: AVECA, 1999.

Alemán, José Luis, S.J. "El proceso de construcción de la nacionalidad dominicana." Included in La República Dominicana en el umbral del siglo XXI: cultura, política y cambio social. Eds. Ramonina Brea, Rosario Espiral, Fernando Valerio-Holguín. Santo Domingo: Pontíficia Universidad Católica Madre y Maestra, 1999.

Álvarez Martín, David. "Crítica de la razón Dominicana." La República Dominicana en el umbral del siglo XXI: cultura, política y cambio social. Ed. Ramonina Brea, Rosario Espiral, Fernando Valerio-Holguín. Santo Domingo: Pontificia Universidad Católica Madre y Maestra, 1999.

Arce, Carmen Vázquez. "Los desastres de la guerra: sobre la articulación de la ironía en los cuentos 'La recién nacida sangre',de Luis Rafael Sánchez y 'El momento divino de Caruso LLompart', de Félix Córdova Iturregui." Revista Iberoamericana. 59 (1993): 162-163.

Arroyo, Elsa R. La contracultura, la parodia y lo grotesco: carnavalización de la literatura en los cuentos de Rosario Ferré y Ana Lydia Vega. Diss. New Brunswick: Rutgers, The State University of New Jersey, 1989.

Bakhtin, M. M. The Dialogic Imagination. Trans. Caryl Emerson and Michael Holquist. Austin: Texas UP, 1981.

Bakhtin, M. M. & Medvedev, P. N. The Formal Method in Literary Scholarship. Trans. Albert J. Wehrle. Baltimore: Johns Hopkins UP, 1991.

Bankay, Anne María. "Contemporary Women Poets of the Dominican Republic: Perspectives on Race and Other Social Issues." Afro-Hispanic Review 12 (Spring 1993): 34.

Baraka, Amiri. Daggers and Javelins. New York: Morrow, 1984.

Benítez-Rojo, Antonio.   The Repeating Island. Trans. James E. Maraniss. Durham: Duke U P, 1996.

Benjamin, Walter. "Theses on the Philosophy of History." Trans. Harry Zohn. Illuminations: Essays and Reflections. Ed. Hannah Arendt. New York: Schocken Books, 1969.

Bhabha, Homi.   "Culture's In-Between."   Included in Questions of Cultural Identity. Hall, Stuart and Paul Du Gay, eds. London: Sage Publications, 1996.

Boadas, Aura Marina & Fernández Merino, Mireya. eds. La huella étnica en la narrativa caribeña. Caracas: Aveca, 1999. Bonachea, Rolando E. and Nelson P. Valdés. Revolutionary Struggle 1947–1958. Cambridge: The MIT Press, 1972.

Brantlinger, Patrick.   Crusoe's Footprints: Cultural Studies in Britain and America. New York: Routledge, 1990.

Brathwaite, Edward Kamau.   "The African Presence in Caribbean Literature." Included in Africa in Latin America. Fraginals, Manuel Moreno, ed. Trans. Leonor Blum. New York: Holmes and Meier Publishers, 1984.

Campbell, Joseph. The Hero With a Thousand Faces. New York: Pantheon Books, 1949.

Capó, Bobby. "El negro bembón." Perf. Celia Cruz. Tributo a Ismael Rivera. New York: Key Productions, 1992.

Carey-Webb, Allen. Making Subject(s):Literature and the Emergence of National Identity. New York: Garland Publishing, 1998.

Cirlot, J. E. A Dictionary of Symbols. Trans. Jack Sage. 2nd ed. New York: Routledge, 1971.

Cohn, Deborah N. History and Memory in the Two Souths: Recent Southern and Spanish American Fiction. Nashville: Vanderbilt UP, 1999.

Cruz, María I. Acosta. "Historia y escritura femenina en Olga Nolla, Magali García Ramis, Rosario Ferré y Ana Lydia Vega." Revista Iberoamericana 59 (1993): 265-277.

Damas, German Carrera. "Flight and Confrontation." Included in Africa in Latin America. Fraginals, Manuel Moreno, ed. Trans. Leonor Blum. New York: Holmes and Meier Publishers, 1984.

Daroqui- María Julia.   (Dis)locaciones: Narrativas híbridas del Caribe hispano. Valencia: Tirant Lo Blanch Libros, 1998.

Dayan, Joan.   Haiti, History, and the Gods.   Berkeley: California UP, 1995.

Davis, Thadious M.   "Expanding the Limits: The Intersection of Race and Region."   Southern Literary Journal 20. 2 (Spring 1988): 3-11.

De Fillipis, Daisy Cocco.   "Dominican Writers at the Crossroads: Reflections on a Conversation in Progress." Included in The Cultures of the Hispanic Caribbean.   Ed. James Conrad and John Perivolaris, Gainsville: U P Florida, 2000.

Deleuze, Gilles and Felix Guattari.   Toward a Minor Literature. Trans. Dana Polan. Minneapolis: Minnesota UP, 1986.
---. "What is a Minor Literature." Mississippi Review 22.3 (Spring 1983): 13-33.

Dubois, W.E.B. The Souls of Black Folks.   New York: New American Library, 1969.

Esteva-Fabregat, Claudio. Mestizaje in Ibero-America. Trans. John Wheat. Tucson: Arizona UP 1995.

Fanon, Frantz. Black Skin, White Mask. Trans. Charles Lam Markmann. New York: Grove Press, 1967.
---. The Wretched of the Earth. Trans. Constance Farrington. New York: Grove Press, 1963.

Ferrer, Ada. Insurgent Cuba: Race, Nation, and Revolution, 1868-1898. Chapel Hill: North Carolina UP, 1999.

Franco, José Luciano. "Mariana and Maceo" Included in Afrocuba an Anthology on Cuban Writing on Race, Politics and Culture. Pérez Sarduy, Pedro and Jean Stubbs,eds. Melbourne: Ocean Press, 1993.

Freire, Paulo. Pedagogy of the Oppressed. Trans. Myra Bergmana Ramos. New York: Seabury Press, 1974.

Galíndez, Jesús de. The Era of Trujillo: Dominican Dictator. Tucson: New Mexico UP, 1973.

Gallagher, Catherine & Stephan Greenblatt. Practicing New Historicism. Chicago: University of Chicago Press, 2000.

Garalzaga, Luis. La interpretación de los símbolos. Hermenéutica y lenguaje en la filosofía actual. Barcelona: Editorial Anthropos, 1990.

García, Myrna. "La narrativa puertorriqueña contemporánea ante la cuestión nacional." Diss. Berkeley: University of California, 1990.

García-Pérez, Gladys Marel. Insurrection and Revolution: Armed Struggle in Cuba, 1952-1959. Trans. Juan Ortega. London: Lynne Rienner Publishers, 1998.

Gelpí, Juan G. Literatura y paternalismo en Puerto Rico. San Juan: Universidad de Puerto Rico, 1993.
Gómez de Avellaneda, Gertrudis. Sab. Madrid: Ediciones Cátedra, 1999.

Gonçalves, Ana Beatriz. Do outro ao EU: elementos de reculturaçao na poesia do brasileiro Olveira Silveira e do dominicano Blas Jiménez. Diss. Austin: University of Texas, 1997.

González-Echevarría, Roberto. The Voice of the Masters: Writing and Authority in Modern Latin American Literature. Austin: Texas UP, 1985.

González, José Luis. Literatura y sociedad en Puerto Rico. México, D.F.:Fondo de Cultura Económica, 1976.

González Pérez, Aníbal. "Puerto Rico." Handbook of Latin American Literature. Ed. David W. Foster, New York: Garland Publishing, Inc. 1997.

González–Wippler, Migene. Santería: magia africana en Latinoamérica. México, D.F.: Editorial Diana, 1976.

Grossberg, Lawrence. "Identity and Cultural Studies: Is That All There Is?" Included in Questions of Cultural Identity. Hall, Stuart and Paul du Gay,eds. London: Sage Publications, 1996.

Guillén, Nicolás. La paloma de vuelo popular. Buenos Aires: Editorial Losada, 1968.

Hartman, Saidiya V. Scenes of Subjection: Terror, Slavery, and Self–Making in Nineteenth–Century America. Oxford: Oxford UP, 1997.

Hegel, G.W.F. Phenomenology of Spirit. Trans. A.V. Miller. Oxford: Clarendon Press, 1977.

Helg, Aline. Our Rightful Share: The Afro-Cuban Struggle for Equality 1886-1912. Chapel Hill: U P North Carolina, 1995.

Howard, Phillip A. Changing History: Afro-Cuban Cabildos and Societies of Color in the Nineteenth Century. Baton Rouge: Louisiana State UP, 1998.

Isaacs, Jorge. María. Madrid: Cátedra, 1998.

Iser, Wolfgang. Prospecting: From Reader Response to Literary Anthropology. Baltimore: Johns Hopkins UP, 1989.
---. The Act of Reading: A Theory of Aesthetic Response. Baltimore: Johns Hopkins UP, 1978.

Jiménez, Blas. Caribe africano en despertar. Santo Domingo: Editora Nuevas Rutas, 1984.
---. Aquí – otro español. Santo Domingo: Editora Taller, 1980.
---. Exigencias de un cimarrón (en sueños). Editora: Taller, Santo Domingo: Editora Taller, 1987.
Jackson, Richard L. Black Writers in Latin America. Albuquerque: New Mexico UP, 1994.
---. Black Literature and Humanism in Latin America. Athens: Georgia UP, 1988.

---. The Black Image in Latin American Literature. Albuquerque: New Mexico UP, 1976.

---. Black Writers and the Hispanic Canon. New York: Twayne Publishers, 1997.

---. "Black Phobia and the White Aesthetic in Spanish American Literature." Hispania 58 (1975): 467-480.

Judson, C. Fred. Cuba and the Revolutionary Myth: The Political Education of the Cuban Rebel Army, 1953-1963. Boulder: Westview Press, 1984.

Kapcia, Antoni. Cuba Island of Dreams. Oxford: Berg, 2000.

Kubayanda, Josaphat B. "Minority Discourse and the African Collective: Some Examples from Latin American and Caribbean Literature." Cultural Critique 6. (Spring 1987): 113-30.

Lewis, Marvin. "Contemporary Afro-Dominican Poetry: The Example of Blas Jiménez." CLA Journal 34.3 (1991): 301-16.

Luis, William. ed. Voices From Under: Black Narrative in Latin America and the Caribbean. Westport: Greenwood, 1984.

Martí, José. Nuestra América. Barcelona: Editorial Ariel, 1970.

Macgaffey, Wyatt and Cliffor R. Barnett. The Twentieth Century Cuba: The Background of the Castro Revolution. New Haven: HRAF Press, 1962.

Maloof, Judy. Ed and Trans. Testimonies of Cuban and Chilean Woman. Lexington: Kentucky UP Press, 1999.

Matigab, Eugenio. Afro–Cuban Religious Experience: Cultural Reflections in Narrative. Gainesville: UP of Florida, 1996.

Medin, Tzvi. Cuba: The Shaping of Revolutionary Consciousness. Boulder: Lynne Reinner Publications, 1990.

Megenney, William W. Cuba y Brasil: Etnohistoria del empleo religioso del lenguaje afroamericano. Miami: Ediciones Universal, 1999.

Memmi, Albert. The Colonized and the Colonizer. Boston: Beacon, 1940.

Métraux, Alfred. Voodoo in Haiti. Trans. Hugo Charteris. New York: Schocken Books, 1972.

Moore, Carlos. Castro, the Blacks and Africa. Los Angeles: Center for Afro-American Studies, 1988.

Morejón, Nancy. "Race and Nation" Included in AfroCuba: An Anthology of Cuban Writing on Race, Politics and Culture. Pérez Sarduy, Pedro and Jean Stubbs, eds. Melbourne: Ocean Press, 1993.
---. Where the Island Sleeps Like a Wing. Trans. Kathleen Weaver. San Francisco: The Black Scholar Press. 1985.
---. La quinta de los molinos. La Habana: Editorial letras Cubanas, 2000.

Moreno Fraginals, Manuel. "Cultural Contributions and Deculturation" Included in Africa in Latin America.

Moreno Fraginals, Manuel, ed. Trans. Leonor Blum. New York: Holmes & Meier Publishers, 1984.

Morrissey, Marietta. Slave Women in the New World: Gender Stratification in the Caribbean. Lawrence: U P of Kansas, 1989.

Nicholls, David. From Dessalines to Duvalier: Race, Colour and National Independence in Haiti. New Brunswick: Rutgers UP, 1996.

Ong, Walter J. Orality and Literacy: The Technologizing of the Word. New York: Routledge, 1988.

Ortíz, Fernando. Cuban Counterpoint: Tobacco and Sugar. Trans. Harriet De Onís. Durham: Duke UP, 1995.

Pagden, Anthony. The Fall of Natural Man: The American Indian and the Origins of Comparative Ethnology. London: Cambridge UP 1982.

Patterson, Orlando. Slavery and Social Death: A Comparative Study. Cambridge: Harvard UP, 1982.

Pérez de La Riva, Juan. Para la historia de las gentes sin historia. Barcelona: Seix Barral, 1975.

Pineda, Gerardo V. "El negro y el arcoiris: diversidad e interacción racial en dos cuentos de V.S. Naipaul." Included in La huella étnica en la narrativa caribeña. Marina Boadas, Ana and Mireya Fernández Merino,eds. Caracas: AVECA, 1999.

Rama, Angel. Transculturación narrativa en América Latina. Montevideo: Arca Editorial, 1974.

Riggan, William. Pícaros, Madmen, Naifs, and Clowns: The Unreliable First-Person Narrator. Norman: Oklahoma UP, 1981.

Roorda, Eric Paul. The Dictator Next Door. Durham: Duke UP, 1998.

Rosario Candelier, Bruno. "Los valores negros en la poesía dominicana." Eme, Eme (1974): 26-66.

Said, Edward W. The World, the Text and the Critic. Cambridge: Harvard UP, 1983.

Santamaría, Haydée. Moncada. Trans. Robert Taber. Secaucus: Lyle Stuart, 1980.

Simons, Geoff. Cuba: From Conquistador to Castro. New York: St. Martins Press, 1996.

Sklodowska, Elzbieta and Ben A. Heller, eds. Roberto Fernández Retamar y los estudios latinoamericanos. Pittsburgh: UP Pittsburgh, 2000.

Smart, Ian Isidore. Nicolás Guillén: Popular Poet of the Caribbean. Columbia: UP of Missouri, 1990.

Sommers, Doris. One Master For Another: Populism as Patriarchal Rhetoric in Dominican Novels. Lanhan: America Up, 1983.

Stuckey, Sterling. Slave Culture: Nationalist Theory and the Foundations of Black America. Oxford: Oxford UP, 1987.

Szanto, George. Narrative Taste and Social Perspectives: The Matter of Quality. London: MacMillan Press, 1987.

Taylor, Patrick. "The Narrative of Liberation: Perspectives on Afro-Caribbean Literature, Popular Culture, and Politics."Afro-Hispanic Review 3 (1989): (20-21).

Torres, Vicente Francisco. La novela bolero latinoamericana. México: UNAM, 1998.

Torres, Arlene and Norman E. Whittern Jr. Blackness in Latin America and the Caribbean: Social Dynamics and Cultural Transformations. Vol II, Bloomington: Indiana UP, 1998.

Vega, Ana Lydia. Vírgenes y mártires. Carolina: Editorial Antillana, 1981.

---. Encancaranublado y otros cuentos de naufragio.

Carolina: Editorial Antillana, 1994.

---. Pasión de historia y otras historias de passion. Buenos Aires: Ediciones de la Flor, 1987.

---. Falsas crónicas del sur. Editorial: UPR, 1991.

---. Esperando a Loló y otros delirios generacionales. Editorial: UPR, 1994.

---. El tramo ancla: ensayos puertorriqueños de hoy. Editorial: UPR, 1989.

Veloz Maggiolo, Marcio. Sobre cultura dominicana y otras culturas: Ensayos. Santo Domingo: Alfa y Omega, 1977: 108.

Villaverde, Cirilo. Cecilia Valdés o la loma del ángel. Caracas: Biblioteca Ayacucho, 1981.

Warnick, Barbara. "Two Systems of Invention: The Topics in the Rhetoric and The New Rhetoric." Included in Rereading Aristotle's Rhetoric. Eds. Alan G. Gross, Arthur E. Walzer. Carbondale: Southern Illinois UP, 2000.

West, Cornel. Prophetic Reflections: Notes on Race and Power in America. Monroe: Common Courage Press, 1993.

---. Keeping Faith: Philosophy and Race in America. New York and London: Routledge, 1993.

---.   Prophecy Deliverance: An Afro-American Revolutionary Christianity.   Philadelphia: Westminster Press, 1982.

Williams, Claudette M.   Charcoal & Cinnamon: The Politics of Color in Spanish Caribbean Literature. Gainsville: UP of Florida, 2000.

Williams, Eric. From Columbus to Castro: The History of the Caribbean 1492-1969. New York: Harper and Row, 1970.

Winn, Peter.   Americas: The Changing Face of Latin America and the Caribbean. Berkeley: California UP, 1995.

Wylie, Hal.   "Negritude and Beyond: The Quest for Identity and Meaning." Included in Interdisciplinary Dimensions of African Literature (1985): 43–51.

Zavala, Iris.   Colonialism and Culture. Bloomington: Indiana UP, 1992.

Zea, Leopoldo.   Dependencia y liberación en la cultura latinoamericana. México: Editorial Joaquín Mortiz, 1974.

Zielina, María Carmen. La africanía en el cuento cubano y puertorriqueño. Miami: Ediciones Universal, 1992.